CAMBRIDGE MUSIC HANDBOOKS

Ives: *Concord Sonata*

CAMBRIDGE MUSIC HANDBOOKS

GENERAL EDITOR Julian Rushton

Cambridge Music Handbooks provide accessible introductions to major
musical works

Published titles

Bach: *The Brandenburg Concertos* MALCOLM BOYD
Bach: Mass in B Minor JOHN BUTT
Bartók: *Concerto for Orchestra* DAVID COOPER
Beethoven: *Missa solemnis* WILLIAM DRABKIN
Beethoven: *Pastoral Symphony* DAVID WYN JONES
Beethoven: Symphony No. 9 NICHOLAS COOK
Berg: Violin Concerto ANTHONY POPLE
Berlioz: *Roméo et Juliette* JULIAN RUSHTON
Brahms: *A German Requiem* MICHAEL MUSGRAVE
Chopin: The Four Ballades JIM SAMSON
Debussy: *La mer* SIMON TREZISE
Handel: *Messiah* DONALD BURROWS
Haydn: *The Creation* NICHOLAS TEMPERLEY
Haydn: String Quartets, Op. 50 W. DEAN SUTCLIFFE
Holst: *The Planets* RICHARD GREENE
Ives: *Concord Sonata* GEOFFREY BLOCK
Janáček: *Glagolitic Mass* PAUL WINGFIELD
Liszt: Sonata in B Minor KENNETH HAMILTON
Mahler: Symphony No. 3 PETER FRANKLIN
Mendelssohn: *The Hebrides* and other overtures R. LARRY TODD
Mozart: Clarinet Concerto COLIN LAWSON
Mozart: The 'Jupiter' Symphony ELAINE R. SISMAN
Musorgsky: *Pictures at an Exhibition* MICHAEL RUSS
Schoenberg: *Pierrot lunaire* JONATHAN DUNSBY
Schubert: *Die schöne Müllerin* SUSAN YOUENS
Schumann: Fantasie, Op. 17 NICHOLAS MARSTON
Sibelius: Symphony No. 5 JAMES HEPOKOSKI
Strauss: *Also sprach Zarathustra* JOHN WILLIAMSON
Stravinsky: *Oedipus rex* STEPHEN WALSH
Verdi: Requiem DAVID ROSEN
Vivaldi: *The Four Seasons* and other concertos, Op. 8 PAUL EVERETT

Ives: *Concord Sonata*

Piano Sonata No. 2
("Concord, Mass., 1840–1860")

Geoffrey Block

Professor of Music
University of Puget Sound

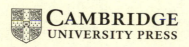

CAMBRIDGE
UNIVERSITY PRESS

Published by the Press Syndicate of the University of Cambridge
The Pitt Building, Trumpington Street, Cambridge CB2 1RP
40 West 20th Street, New York, NY 10011–4211, USA
10 Stamford Road, Oakleigh, Melbourne 3166, Australia

First published 1996

Printed in Great Britain at the University Press, Cambridge

A catalogue record for this book is available from the British Library

Library of Congress cataloguing in publication data

Block, Geoffrey Holden.
Ives, *Concord sonata*: piano sonata no. 2 ("Concord, Mass.,
1840–1860") / Geoffrey Block.
p. cm. – (Cambridge music handbooks)
Includes bibliographical references and index.
ISBN 0 521 49656 X (hardback) – ISBN 0 521 49821 X (paperback)
1. Ives, Charles, 1874–1954. Sonatas, piano, no. 2. I. Title.
II. Series.
ML410.I94B56   1996
786.2'183–dc20 95–46934 CIP MN

ISBN 0 521 49656 X hardback
ISBN 0 521 49821 X paperback

SE

3366474

For *my* "two little flowers"
Jessamyn and Eliza

and for Jacqueline
the sun that nourishes them

On sunny days in our back yard,
Two little flowers are seen,
One dressed, at times, in brightest pink
And one in green.

The marigold is radiant,
The rose passing fair;
The violet is ever dear,
The orchid ever rare;

There's loveliness in wild flowers
Of field or wide savannah,
But fairest, rarest of them all
Are Edith and Susanna.

Two Little Flowers (and dedicated to them)
(text by Charles and Harmony Ives, 1921)

FROM NINETEEN SONGS
© 1935 Merion Music, Inc.
Used By Permission Of The Publisher
Theodore Presser Company

Contents

Contents

Musical examples

Acknowledgements

The University of Puget Sound generously granted me a sabbatical enhancement award that allowed me an uninterrupted opportunity to complete this labor of joy. Kendall Crilly and the staff of the Yale University Music Library provided helpful and friendly assistance in locating and using source materials. Thomas M. Brodhead, Gayle Sherwood, and James B. Sinclair shared their time and the fruits of their indispensable work (in several instances in advance of publication), especially on the intricacies of Ives's chronology and compositional process. I am very grateful to series editor Julian Rushton for reading the manuscript swiftly, yet carefully, and for suggesting the Berlioz reference at the conclusion of chapter 6. Thanks also to Andrea B. Smith for her helpful copy-editing, to Kathryn Puffet for her meticulous music-setting, and to Penny Souster of Cambridge University Press for her advice and support. The dedicatees of this volume, my wife, Jacqueline, and my "two little flowers" (to borrow an Ives song title), Jessamyn and our newborn Eliza, created an environment of love and rebirth at a time when I was losing (then lost) my best friend, John Boswell. Above all, I cannot thank J. Peter Burkholder enough (but will try nonetheless) for his thorough and meticulous reading of an earlier draft and his copiously helpful suggestions both large and small, for setting a new standard with his inspiring previously published work on Ives and for sharing his monumental *All Made of Tunes* (Yale University Press, 1995) several years prior to its publication, and for encouraging my own Ives projects at every stage.

Special thanks to the following individuals and institutions for permitting me to reprint their holdings: Yale University Music Library (cover photograph from the Charles Ives Papers); Thomas Broido, President,

Theodore Presser Co., (Charles and Harmony Ives's song text, *Two Little Flowers*); and Zoraya Mendez-DeCosmis, Print Licensing Manager, Associated Music Publishers, Inc. (*Concord Sonata* music examples). The copyright designation for the latter is Copyright © 1947, 1976 (Renewed) by Associated Music Publishers, Inc. (BMI) International Copyright Secured. All Rights Reserved. Reprinted by Permission.

1

Introduction

Following Henry Bellamann's laudatory review in 1921, the *Concord Sonata* has been increasingly recognized as a significant work, both in Ives's compositional output and in American music as a whole.[1] Among the last completed large-scale compositions of Ives's maturity, the *Concord Sonata* is further distinguished as the only composition for which Ives was motivated to prepare and distribute book-length program notes and as the first work the composer chose to publish at his own expense. This latter decision has considerably skewed the reception history of this unusual composer's music. As J. Peter Burkholder writes, "Ives is the only major composer whose works have come to light in approximately reverse chronological order, beginning with his latest, most difficult, and most idiosyncratic pieces."[2]

Nearly twenty years after Bellamann's review, the *Concord Sonata*, an important representative of Ives's late, difficult, and idiosyncratic compositions, acquired additional notoriety when it received its second unequivocally positive critical review in response to its Town Hall performance by John Kirkpatrick (1905–91) in 1939. Although the sonata had been formerly ridiculed almost without exception as unplayable, amateurish, and unreasonably modern, more than one influential critic was now prepared to extol the work as containing "music as beautiful at the very least as any composed by an American" or even as "the greatest music composed by an American."[3] Eight years later in 1947 the *Concord Sonata* became Ives's first multi-movement composition to appear in a revised second edition (unless otherwise noted, all page references in the present handbook will be keyed to this second edition, published by Associated Music Publishers).[4] With the release of Kirkpatrick's performance on Columbia Records the following year the *Concord Sonata* earned an additional historical accolade when it became the first major Ives composition to be released on a prestigious label.[5]

Its unmistakable linkage to the Concord Transcendentalists, Emerson and Thoreau, gave the *Concord Sonata* an aura and a cachet, especially for listeners unable to fully negotiate Ives's complex *musical* realization of this familiar and authentically American programmatic subject. Perhaps anticipating this possibility, on the dedication page of the *Essays Before a Sonata* Ives wrote that his "prefatory essays were written by the composer for those who can't stand his music."[6] For these dedicatees, the *Concord Sonata* contains by far the most wide-ranging and occasionally detailed philosophical and programmatic introduction of any work by this (or perhaps any other) composer. Despite the occasionally impenetrable difficulties posed by his prose, Ives's *Essays* also offer many quotable and provocative references adding to the mystique of this iconoclastic American composer and his *Concord Sonata*, for example: "Beauty in music is too often confused with something that lets the ears lie back in an easy chair" and perhaps most famously, "My God! What has sound got to do with music!" (*Essays*, pp. 97 and 84).

In addition to the work's intrinsic merits, the relatively accessible programmatic content and literary connections presented in the *Essays* no doubt helped make the *Concord Sonata* a frequent and usually honored guest in historical surveys of American music with appearances beginning the year after Ives's death in Gilbert Chase's influential *America's Music: From the Pilgrims to the Present* (1955).[7] Specialized studies on Ives have similarly featured the *Concord Sonata*. From Sidney and Henry Cowell's pioneering life and works (published the same year as Chase's survey) to studies by Stuart Feder and Wolfgang Rathert in the 1990s, Ives scholars generally consider the *Concord Sonata* a work of central importance in his output and a work of historical and artistic significance in American music.[8]

The vast attention devoted to the *Concord Sonata*, including two monographs devoted solely to the work and dozens of chapters and essays in which it figures prominently, makes it fruitless to attempt a comprehensive examination in a volume of this type.[9] Instead, the present handbook will focus on a few topics chosen to serve readers who are unfamiliar with either Ives or his *Concord Sonata* as well as scholars and performers looking for a compendium of information that incorporates recent findings. Areas to be explored in chapters 2–6 include reception history, compositional genesis, form and design, musical borrowing, and programmaticism. This introduction will conclude with a few preliminary remarks on each.

For the world at large the story of the *Concord Sonata* begins near the end of Ives's active life as a composer. Chapter 2 thus begins in January 1921 (*Memos*, p. 163) when for the first time, Ives sent out into the world a major musical work, along with an accompanying volume of essays, both of which had been printed privately at the composer's expense several months earlier. During the next two decades Ives would acquire a series of musical champions beginning with Henry Bellamann, E. Robert Schmitz, Henry Cowell, and Nicholas Slonimsky in the 1920s and continuing with Aaron Copland, Lehman Engel, Lou Harrison, and Leonard Bernstein among others in the 1930s, '40s, and '50s. All the members of this illustrious list worked to varying degrees and with varying success on Ives's behalf to promote the avant-garde and later the somewhat more conventional (and even tonal) music that also incorporated authentic American literary and musical themes.[10] Most crucial for the discovery and dissemination of the *Concord Sonata* were the efforts of Kirkpatrick, first with his pioneering performances in 1938 and 1939 and later with the exercise of his profound knowledge of the work and its sources and his unfailing generosity to younger Ives scholars. Despite the nearly twenty recordings and considerable attention it has received in academic circles, however, the *Concord Sonata* remains a "difficult" work, like other comparable modernist compositions more talked about than listened to or performed, but a work nonetheless widely recognized as a twentieth-century masterpiece.

Chapter 3 moves backward in time to the decade of compositional genesis that preceded the work's completion in 1919 and distribution in 1921. Such a study requires the re-examination of the *Concord Sonata* chronology offered by the composer (*Memos*, pp. 79–83, 150, 162–63, and 185–204). Until the late 1980s Ives's chronology was invariably adopted by scholars, including (despite some reservations) Kirkpatrick. Elliott Carter's 1939 challenge to the precociousness and priority of Ives's musical innovations (with its corollary accusation that Ives added dissonance retrospectively) was not taken up again until Maynard Solomon's 1987 essay in the *Journal of the American Musicological*

Society.[11] Prior to Solomon's revisionist stance, Ives's anticipation of twentieth-century techniques and practices (polytonality, serialism, and aleatory music to name three out of the many attributed to him) was taken as gospel. For some critics and scholars, such precociousness served to justify Ives's artistic as well as historical importance. Following the vigorous challenge posed by Solomon, the work of a new generation of scholars led by Gayle Sherwood has precipitated some revised chronological conclusions based on the examination of paper types and handwriting characteristics.[12]

In applying Sherwood's methodologies to the *Concord Sonata*, and through an independent examination of manuscript sources, the present handbook offers a genesis that differs in some respects from that offered by the composer. Most importantly, the manuscript evidence suggests that the version of the *Concord Sonata* Ives performed for his friend Max Smith in 1912 was probably incomplete and that much of the sonata first printed in 1920 was composed between 1915–19 rather than between 1911–15 as earlier supposed. On the other hand, although Ives did in fact add dissonances after 1920, a considerable number of these are more accurately a *return* to dissonances already present in the incomplete *Emerson Overture* (abandoned about 1911) or the 1919 ink autograph.[13]

In its adherence to traditional principles of thematic construction, the *Concord Sonata*, like other Ives works from various periods of his career, can, despite its modernity, be viewed as a composition with strong ties to nineteenth-century predecessors from Beethoven and Schubert to Wagner and Strauss. While motivic analysis has been challenged as the dominant analytical paradigm in recent decades, the fact remains that Ives conceived and executed his sonata as an intricate intertwining mosaic of related motives, combinations of motives, and inexhaustible transformations in both manner and substance. The narrative of the *Concord Sonata*'s motivic content outlined in chapter 4 reflects the importance of Ives's melodic manipulation in this work. An index of the *Concord Sonata* themes and an encapsulated formal and thematic outline can be found in Appendixes 1 and 2, respectively.

Ives's pervasive practice of musical borrowing has been both criticized for its naiveté and praised for its sophistication.[14] The chapter on borrowing will survey the history of attributions from the certifiable to the hypothetical. One of the biases implicitly underlying chapter 5 is that Ives's use of borrowed material, rather than reflecting a poverty of musical invention, reveals a composer rich in sophistication, skill, and imagination.

Even when motivated primarily by musical rather than programmatic concerns, few of Ives's borrowing choices were accidental or capricious. Further, Beethoven, the composer whose Fifth Symphony (Appendix 1, theme 7) and "Hammerklavier" Sonata (theme 9) occupy the musical and spiritual center of the *Concord Sonata*, was a composer who exerted a strong and acknowledged "anxiety of influence" on Ives. Only in the mature *Concord Sonata*, however, was Ives able to confront Beethoven, to convert the "sounds that Beethoven didn't have" (*Memos*, p. 44) into his own personal modernist musical language, and to successfully combine eulogy and critique.[15] A symbol of excellence and spirituality in the European classical tradition for the Concord Transcendentalists, Beethoven also served as a fitting patriarch for a family of themes (Ex. 4.1, a–g) and the principal musical subject for a sonata based at least partly on Transcendentalism. The still-popular Stephen Foster, who served as an example of America's musical greatness beginning with the boyhood of Ives's revered father, provided another foundation as a vernacular patriarch who could represent Ives's second family of themes (Ex. 4.2, a–f).

Similarly, Ives's choice of principal hymns and popular music, many of which were doubtless chosen for the musical qualities they share with Beethoven's Fifth Symphony and "Hammerklavier," successfully links Ives's world to that of the Concord writers working between 1840–60 and the music of their day.[16] In fact, the hymns, classical references (other than Beethoven), and popular borrowings viewed in this handbook as reasonable attributions, were nearly all composed between 1840 and 1860. In chronological order they include: Simeon B. Marsh's *Martyn* (1834); Charles Zeuner's *Missionary Chant* (1834); David T. Shaw's "Columbia, the Gem of the Ocean" (1843); Anthony F. Winnemore's "Stop That Knocking at My Door" (1843); Richard Wagner's *Wedding March* from *Lohengrin* (premiered, 1850); the anonymous *Crusader's Hymn* (arranged by Richard S. Willis, 1850); and Foster's "Massa's in De Cold Ground" (1852).[17] Wagner's *Prelude* to *Tristan und Isolde* (Appendix 1, theme 11), one of several borrowings suggested for the first time in this handbook as arguably genuine, received its premiere in 1865.

After a period of denial, programmaticism is no longer so readily dismissed as irrelevant to our understanding of a composition and is again being taken seriously in musicological circles.[18] Nevertheless, the dissonance between Kurt Stone's and Gordon Cyr's interpretation of Ives's Fourth Symphony, which might also be applied to the *Concord Sonata*, has by no means been resolved.[19] For Stone, Ives's tunes exhibit "no apparent musical relevance to the whole of the work," while Cyr finds "a perfectly valid *musical* justification for the various movements' character." For those who view programmaticism as an oil spill upon pure musical waters, the present handbook preserves a somewhat artificial separation between the program and the music. The middle ground adopted here is that not all the music in the *Concord Sonata* can be accounted for programmatically, even by conflating all of Ives's direct and reported observations on this subject. Conversely, considerable portions of the programmatic content cannot be accounted for in the music itself.

Chapter 6 on Ives's philosophical and narrative program explores his approach to Transcendentalism based on selective reading – Harold Bloom might even say misreading – of the Concord writers. It also attempts to show how some of these views might be manifest in the *Concord Sonata*. As Burkholder has shown, while writers since the 1930s have tried to force the music into a Transcendentalist mold, much of Ives's interpretation of Transcendentalism, like his musical language, is idiosyncratic and personal.[20] For this reason, the present handbook eschews the customary commentary on the relationship, often forced, between Ives and the nineteenth-century philosophical tradition in favor of an examination of Ives's personal vision of four literary subjects associated with the town of Concord between 1840 and 1860. Significantly, these years correspond to the formative decades in the life of Ives's father, George (1845–94).[21]

Although this handbook will try to make Ives's formidable sonata more accessible, or at least more comprehensible, it would be a fool's errand to attempt to reconcile fully its contradictions and heterogeneities, to simplify its complexities, or to soften its dissonances. In any event, this volume is governed by the premise that the *Concord Sonata* is one work that definitely does need an introduction. It is also hoped that this handbook will contribute to a greater acceptance and admiration of this remarkable composition and perhaps even pleasure and delight in Ives's craft, intuition, and idealism.

2

Reception

Critical responses 1920–1938

Remarkably, the *Concord Sonata* was the first work Ives had offered to the public since five short compositions were published in 1896 and 1897 during his college days at Yale University. Throughout the intervening years, Ives's most active composing years, few subsequent works were even rehearsed by professional musicians. When Ives's *magnum opus* (or at least a strong candidate for this distinction), the *Concord Sonata*, along with its elaborate philosophical program notes, the *Essays Before a Sonata*, arrived unannounced and unheralded to *Musical Courier* subscribers and other musicians in 1921, Ives was virtually unknown.

Within a few months after Ives began to distribute his *Essays* and sonata in January 1921 the pair of offerings was reviewed briefly and condescendingly in two established music journals, the *Musical Courier* and *Musical America*.[1] Both reviews commented derisively on Ives's perspicacity in enclosing a slip that reads "Complimentary: copies are not to be sold." "At last a composer who realizes the unsalable quality of his music," wrote A. Walter Kramer in *Musical America*. The anonymous *Musical Courier* reviewer similarly remarked with assurance that Ives's fear of profiting from his work was psychosomatic.

Each reviewer quoted and responded to Ives's self-deprecatory preface: "These prefatory essays were written by the composer for those who can't stand his music – and the music for those who can't stand his essays; to those who can't stand either, the whole is respectfully dedicated."[2] The *Musical Courier* replied that no one will be able to react to the music, "for nobody else [other than perhaps the composer] will ever be able to play it for us, since the musical nomenclature of Charles [sic] is entirely a personal affair." Still more sarcastically, *Musical America* respectfully accepted Ives's dedication by stating emphatically, *"We can't stand either."*[3]

Each of the five published responses to the *Concord Sonata* in 1921 commented on the difficulty of the work, either as a consequence of its dissonant musical language, its unplayability, or its lack of professionalism, criticisms that more than seventy-five years have not entirely vanquished. The "not easily taken aback" Ernest Walker, writing in the then fledgling journal *Music & Letters*, wrote that the *Concord Sonata* "may be safely recommended as a tonic to anyone bored with the reactionary conservatism of European extremists."[4] Walker singles out for dubious originality "the simultaneous pounding of the piano by both clenched fists (an interesting effect best practised on someone else's instrument)," the infamous strip of board in "Hawthorne," and the "bewildering notation." In an early indictment of Ives's stylistic heterogeneity, Walker also criticizes the "two percent" of the work that presents "the plainest common chords that sound exactly like a beginner's first attempts at harmony exercises" as well as the normative highly dissonant style familiar "in households where the baby or the cat has access to the piano."

Musical America considered the work "without any doubt the most startling conglomeration of meaningless notes that we have ever seen engraved on white paper" (even more than Béla Bartók's Second String Quartet or the songs of Lord Berners). For Edwin J. Stringham, writing in Denver's *Rocky Mountain News*, Ives "surpasses" "in cacophony" the "strange music" written by Igor Stravinsky, Arnold Schoenberg, Leo Ornstein, and Alfredo Casella.[5] Stringham, who received a personal response from Ives "concerning his ideals and training," concluded that the composer "essentially is a humorist," a composer "having a good time making sport of the 'cubistic' type of music." Why else would a composer who "has had the advantage of exceptional musical training" write such music? "The jump from Bach to the 'Concord' is too great in difference to be true – at least serious."

Unlike the *Musical Courier* and *Musical America* reviewers, neither of whom could "stand" the sonata or the *Essays*, Stringham was more charitable towards the literary component of Ives's package, conceding that "some of the composer's statements are witty, informative and make unusually fascinating reading." In a similar vein Ernest Walker observed that "some of the few pages that are in any way concerned with music have good sense under their verbiage."

The most detailed response to Ives's unsolicited distribution of his *Essays* and his sonata came from Henry Bellamann, two decades later the author of the enormously successfully novel, *King's Row* (1940).[6] Unlike all the other early reviewers, Bellamann, then the Dean of Fine Arts at Chicora College for Women in Columbia, South Carolina, found much to praise in both Ives's literary and musical efforts and published an extended laudatory review in the *Double Dealer*, a new journal based in New Orleans. Through correspondence with Ives, Bellamann, like Stringham, was able to incorporate into his review additional biographical and other materials related to what Ives was trying to accomplish.

In stark contrast to the reviews in *Musical Courier*, *Musical America*, *Music & Letters*, and the *Rocky Mountain News*, Bellamann took Ives's originality seriously and viewed the sonata as "a piece of work sincerely done." He also made several prescient observations that would be associated with Ives and his sonata for decades to follow. Although later in the review he acknowledges a superficial *visual* similarity with Richard Strauss, Bellamann does not swerve from his earlier conclusion that the *Concord Sonata* "reveals music unlike anything one has seen before – a broad, strong and original style with no recognizable derivations from Debussy, Strauss or Strawinsky." Such statements anticipated and perhaps contributed to the establishment of a mythological Ives, an American uninfluenced by the courtly muses of Europe. Like other Ivesian myths, the image of the isolated composer was aided and abetted by the composer himself, and is still often encountered despite rigorous recent challenges.[7] Bellamann concluded his review in the *Double Dealer* with a tribute to the *Concord Sonata*'s abstract "loftiness of purpose" with "moments of achievement elevating and greatly beautiful."

Ives's predilection for an assistant pianist implicit in his correspondence with Bellamann (quoted in the review) that the sonata "was not written primarily to be played – certainly not to be played with two hands" gave rise to a body of writing that viewed the work, again following Ives's lead, as "an experiment which perhaps goes too far."[8] The infamous board of wood on page 25 (both editions), the tone clusters on page 40 (first edition) [page 41 in the second] in "Hawthorne," and the absence of bar lines throughout further contributed to the impression that Ives was bypassing "familiar pianistic outlines" in favor of orchestral writing.[9] Perhaps surprisingly, Bellamann considered "Thoreau" "more difficult to understand than the Emerson movement, certainly more difficult to play," although, paradoxically, at the same time he judged the final movement "more pianistically playable." In contrast to Ives, who like Thoreau, decidedly preferred to hear the flute over Walden, Bellamann espoused the opinion later steadfastly maintained by John Kirkpatrick that the entrance of the flute on the final pages of the "Thoreau" movement was "an abstraction" which "breaks the mood."[10]

In addition to Bellamann, Ives's beloved and perhaps biased former English professor William Lyon Phelps generously wrote in the *Yale Alumni Weekly* that he "enjoyed every page" of the *Essays* and that Ives had written "a brilliant and provocative book, full of challenging ideas, and marked by chronic cerebration."[11] Private sympathetic responses were also received from two distinguished music professors unknown to Ives, Percy Goetschius of Columbia University and Clarence G. Hamilton of Wellesley College, both of whom, in Ives's view at least, partially eschewed the "persistent fundamental misunderstanding" exhibited by most recipients.[12] More representative are the hostile and condescending letters from the composer Charles Wakefield Cadman and Harmony Ives's former personal friend, the patroness Elizabeth Sprague Coolidge.[13]

After these initial public and private responses, the *Concord Sonata* was rarely and incompletely heard in professional concerts or discussed in print until Kirkpatrick's premiere performance in 1939. In 1921 Clifton Furness presented "The Alcotts" in a lecture-recital and discussed the sonata in his courses at Northwestern University.[14] In 1921 and 1922 Bellamann organized and presented lecture-recitals in Columbia, South Carolina and Atlanta in which portions of the sonata were performed by Lenore Purcell.[15] Other early performances of various movements took place in Salzburg where Oscar Ziegler performed "The Alcotts" in 1928; the same year and the next Keith Corelli played "Emerson" in several Southern and Western states (*Memos*, pp. 201 and 237, n. 10).

Despite the psychological benefits his early positive recognition offered, Bellamann lacked the musical contacts to ensure professional performances and publications of Ives's music. The first professional musician to play this role in a drama that would raise the stature of an unknown composer to near canonization within a span of three to four decades was E. Robert Schmitz, the eminent French pianist who in 1920 founded the Franco-American Musical Society (renamed the Pro Musica in 1923). Whether he actually received the sonata is uncertain, but it is known that Schmitz was on Ives's list of intended recipients in 1921 and that he first met Ives in 1923.[16] Schmitz, like Henry Cowell in the late 1920s, responded most favorably to Ives's avant-garde compositions and arranged for Pro Musica performances at Aeolian Hall in 1925 of the *Chorale* and *Allegro* from the *Three Quarter-Tone Pieces* and the first two movements of the Fourth Symphony at Town Hall two years later. In 1929 Cowell, with indispensable financial assistance from Ives, published the second movement of this symphony in his newly established *New Music Quarterly.*

Cowell's eager solicitation of the *Concord Sonata* did not lead to its publication in *New Music*, but several other Ives scores would appear in this avant-garde journal over the next three decades.[17] Cowell also introduced Ives to Nicholas Slonimsky, who in 1931 conducted the premiere of *Three Places in New England* in New York City's Town Hall and in Paris. The following year Ives gained recognition with a broader musical establishment when Aaron Copland organized and accompanied seven Ives songs, including *Charlie Rutlage*, at a festival at Yaddo in Saratoga Springs, New York.

All this activity in the late 1920s and early 1930s set the stage for the future recognition of Ives as an American composer of major interest. The year of the Fourth Symphony premiere Kirkpatrick, then a young American pianist in Paris, discovered Katherine Ruth Heyman's copy of the *Concord Sonata* and began his gradual "penetration" of the work (*Memos*, p. 198).[18] The year Ives's songs were performed at Yaddo, Kirkpatrick was playing "The Alcotts." In 1934 he decided to learn the entire sonata and established communication with the composer, and by 1935 he was playing "Emerson."

Before his historic public debut of the *Concord Sonata* in Town Hall on January 20, 1939 Kirkpatrick tested the work in private and semipublic lecture-recitals the previous June and November. The second of these events, which took place at the "Old House" in Cos Cob, Connecticut, was reviewed with extraordinary sympathy by Paul Rosenfeld in

Modern Music in the issue that preceded Elliott Carter's more widely circulated mixed review.[19] As early as 1932 Rosenfeld had proclaimed Ives "as one of the few originally gifted composers of impressionistic or imitative music borne by America."[20] Two years before the Cos Cob performance Rosenfeld praised Ives's sonata as "the solidest piece of piano music composed by an American."[21]

In his 1938 review Rosenfeld described a structure "Beethoven-like in breadth of conception and cyclic" with "a pair of melodic germs" (the Beethoven Fifth Symphony motive and an unidentified "tender, wooing, chromatic little subject") that link the four movements.[22] He also noted Ives's stylistic heterogeneity, "tonal in spots, polytonal in others and in still others perfectly atonal." Together these competing approaches form "a subtle, sometimes a trifle coarse but oftentimes exquisitely drawn web of these thematic and melodic wisps" (both classical and "folk-song-like"). Rosenfeld did not hesitate to describe Ives's sonata as "melodious with a subtlety not incomparable to that of Debussy or Schoenberg . . . in which every note during entire pages is rhapsodically alive, tremulously expressive, fraught with special poetic emphasis and meaning." Echoing his 1936 epiphany, at the outset of his 1938 review Rosenfeld praised the sonata as "possibly the most intense and sensitive musical experience achieved by an American"; later he espouses his conviction that the "Thoreau" movement presents "music as beautiful at the very least as any composed by an American."

1939 and after

Kirkpatrick's January 1939 premiere performance in a truly public forum, New York City's Town Hall, inspired a review of comparable praise by someone arguably still more influential than Rosenfeld, *New York Herald Tribune*'s first-string music critic, Lawrence Gilman.[23] Like many subsequent critics and historians, Gilman, who had borrowed a copy of Ives's sonata to prepare for the event, found the degree and the priority of Ives's modernism especially significant. Not only does Ives's dissonance and complexity make Schoenberg sound as conservative as Joseph Haydn, Ives had created some of this music in the 1890s when his exact contemporary was exhibiting his "adolescent Wagnerism" and "the youthful Stravinsky was playing marbles in Oranienbaum." In an aesthetic position that would remain a source of evolution until the post-modern era, for Gilman, Ives's greatness was largely due to its precocious and thorough modernity.

Gilman focused his review almost entirely, however, on the timely literary and programmatic features of the work, partially attributable to Van Wyck Brooks's best-selling Pulitzer Prize-winning evocation of the Concord Transcendentalists, *The Flowering of New England*, published three years earlier.[24] Towards the end of the review Gilman praised Ives's music in words that would mark a new phase in the reception of Ives's music and his future casting in the role of "America's Greatest Composer":

> This sonata is exceptionally great music – it is, indeed, the greatest music composed by an American, and the most deeply and essentially American in impulse and implication. It is wide-ranging and capacious. It has passion, tenderness, humor, simplicity, homeliness. It has imaginative and spiritual vastness. It has wisdom and beauty and profoundity [sic], and a sense of the encompassing terror and splendor of human life and human destiny – a sense of those mysteries that are both human and divine.

For Gilman, Ives's sonata was American "music worthy of the great and mystical saying of Emerson himself: that the essence of all things 'is not wisdom, or love, or beauty, . . . but all in one, and each entirely.'"[25]

As a direct consequence of Gilman's January review and public request for an encore, Kirkpatrick repeated the *Concord Sonata* in a second Town Hall recital one month later on February 24, 1939.[26] Although the *New York Times* and the *Musical Courier* overlooked the historic Town Hall premiere in January, Kirkpatrick's return engagement was reviewed by Irving Kolodin in the *New York Sun*, John Sebastian (*nom de plume* for Goddard Lieberson) in *New Masses*, Robert A. Simon in the *New Yorker*, and an anonymous reviewer for *Time*. Kolodin offered praise and criticism that still haunt Ives's reputation, praise for Ives's "amazing perception" in anticipating twentieth-century techniques, criticism for Ives's "lack of discipline" and "inability to distinguish between the gold and the dross that issued from his imagination."[27] As much as he extols the work Sebastian (Lieberson) chastises the art establishment for keeping Ives's sonata, by 1939 nearly two decades old, "imprisoned in an obscurity which amounts to criminal neglect."[28] Even more than Rosenfeld, Lieberson revels in Ives's stylistic heterogeneity, finding a unity behind a seemingly staggering array of diversity, nearly four decades before this controversial characteristic of Ives's music would be more thoroughly defended and appreciated.[29] Simon concludes that "Mr. Ives' compositions won't appear so strange when one gets to listen to them frequently, and more performances seem to be in order."[30] And even in a profile that emphasized such newsworthy stories as Ives's quirky double life and "his horror of publicity," *Time* begrudgingly recognized that Ives is regarded "even by conservative critics as one of the most individual and authentically American of all U.S. composers."[31]

To review Kirkpatrick's command performance in February the *New York Times* sent their first-string reviewer Olin Downes. Downes praised Ives's individuality and "interesting ideas," but could not comprehend "its structural form" and was consequently unable "to come to a definite conclusion about such music." *Modern Music* sent Elliott Carter, who, while a student of Clifton Furness at the Horace Mann School for Boys in New York in the mid-1920s, had been befriended by Ives.[32]

Carter's review was the first in a long series of published reviews, essays, and personal reminiscences in which the younger composer revealed evolving and frequently contradictory opinions regarding his former mentor. Because he had observed Ives adding dissonances to the chamber version of *Putnam's Camp* from *Three Places in New England* a decade earlier, Carter wrote in 1939 that Ives's innovations are exaggerated because of his practice of adding dissonances and polyrhythms years after the alleged completion of a work. Although Carter found "much good in the sonata," he concluded that the work is "more often original than good." He also emphasized the absence of logic, the naive use of quotation, and especially the formal weaknesses, objections that, following Carter's lead, would continue to be leveled at Ives by future critics.

Throughout these writings Carter would remain adamantly opposed to the practice and the effect of Ives's uses of borrowed music. Similarly, the "extreme heterogeneity" of Ives's music contradicted and thereby was destined to disappoint Schoenberg's call for "inner cohesion."[33] On the other hand, Carter would demonstrate a growing appreciation for

Ives's innovative polyrhythmic practices and "multiple layering."[34] More significantly, in an interview published in 1971 Carter altered his original view of the *Concord Sonata* considerably when he admitted Ives to the pantheon of "organic" composers in the Beethoven tradition.[35] More than thirty years after his negative 1939 assessment, Carter concluded that the motivic and harmonic materials of the "Emerson" movement are "highly organized" and "closely interconnected."

The critical attention in major New York newspapers and more specialized music journals devoted to the 1939 premiere, both negative and positive, added considerably to the recognition and prestige of the *Concord Sonata* and its composer. It also created a market for a reprinted or revised edition.[36] Proofs of the latter were ready by 1941, although it did not appear until 1947. One year later Columbia released Kirkpatrick's performance of the work (recorded in April 1945), like all future recordings, including Kirkpatrick's, based for the most part on the second edition.[37]

Also in 1947 Ives gained additional prominence when he received a Pulitzer Prize in music for his Third Symphony. One year after the Columbia recording was released, William Masselos premiered the equally formidable First Piano Sonata. In 1951 Leonard Bernstein conducted the debut of the Second Symphony with the New York Philharmonic, the first of many Ives performances and other public advocacies on the composer's behalf over the next four decades.[38]

By the time Ives died in 1954 the seeds of the "Ives Legend" were firmly planted. The next year Kirkpatrick embarked on the arduous five-year task of identifying and cataloguing thousands of haphazardly stored manuscript pages which were rescued from Ives's West Redding barn and donated to Yale University by Harmony Ives. Also in 1955 the first biography of the composer, written collaboratively by Sidney Cowell (life) and Henry Cowell (music) while Ives was alive, unreservedly placed Ives's stature among the four major composers of the century along with Stravinsky, Schoenberg, and Bartók.[39]

Henry Cowell treated the *Concord Sonata* as a centerpiece in the "works" portion of this first life and works study, and his commentary marked a starting point for subsequent analytical discussions.[40] Not surprisingly, Cowell, the pioneer of the tone cluster, sympathetically singles out to defend and praise such avant-garde elements as the strip of board introduced on page 25 of "Hawthorne." Cowell's primary analytical concern, however, is Ives's motivic unity and his unique approach to organicism within the framework of the classical tradition:

> As is the case with all well-constructed sonatas, all the materials out of which the whole of the rest of the work is to be built can be found in the first measure of the *Concord Sonata*. The rhythmic and thematic development is more involved than in classic examples, but it is of the same general sort, of course with the important exception that it does not proceed from the simple to the complex, but the reverse.[41]

In the first full-scale text on American music, Gilbert Chase's *America's Music*, which appeared the same year as the Cowells', Ives, like Beethoven in most surveys of European music, ranks as the only figure to merit a chapter of his own.[42] In the first two editions of Chase's survey, the *Concord Sonata* received considerable space (ten pages in the 1966 edition), albeit with an almost exclusive emphasis on its programmatic features. More recently, in the 1988 third edition of *Music in the United States* (first published in 1968), H. Wiley Hitchcock offers "no apologies for devoting an entire chapter of a rather brief book to Charles Ives."[43] Hitchcock continues: "Both his thought and his music stand as continuing, fertile challenges to American musical evolution."

In 1964 Wilfrid Mellers, who had been extolling Ives's importance and often his virtues since 1939, devoted nine pages to the *Concord Sonata* in the Ives chapter of his survey *Music in a New Found Land*.[44] According to Mellers, Ives represents "a New World's stumbling approach to a figure of Beethovenian power: which is enough to ensure his place in history." For Mellers, "if one had to choose one work which most effectively embodied Ives's lifelong search it would probably be the tremendous [*Concord*] piano sonata." Borrowing Henry Cowell's terms "lyric" (Appendix 1, theme 3) and "epic" (the Beethoven Fifth Symphony motive, theme 7), among other analytical observations, to describe the two principal themes, Mellers, like Cowell before him, emphasizes the organic nature of Ives's motivic unity: "His themes are always growing, and change their identities as they are related in wildly opposed rhythms or on separate (polytonal) planes of harmony."

Mellers ultimately considers the *Concord Sonata* lacking the "lyrical efflorescence" of the Arietta from Beethoven's opus 111, and views

Ives's sonata as "of course a much less significant piece" than Beethoven's "Hammerklavier" Sonata, op. 106. Nevertheless, the frequent comparisons between Ives and Beethoven (middle and late, no less) throughout his discussion suggest that for Mellers, Ives is one American composer who can be readily compared to this European giant.

Concurrently with the Ives Centennial in 1974 (billed as "the first international congress ever dedicated to an American composer") and the chauvinism of the American Bicentennial was an escalation in Ives's critical and scholarly prestige as well as a proliferation of public performances and recordings. Figuring prominently in all this attention were dozens of articles and reviews on the *Concord Sonata* in popular and scholarly journals of all types, dissertations, chapters of books, and even whole monographs (see the Bibliography).

Nine years after its 1980 publication in German, English readers would read the revered German musicologist Carl Dahlhaus's description of the *Concord Sonata* as "random accumulation of dissonance."[45] Nevertheless, by the time *Music in the New World* appeared in 1983, the American musicologist Charles Hamm could write that "enough has been written about the *Concord Sonata* elsewhere to make it unnecessary to continue here."[46] Confirming that this new neglect did not signify contempt, Hamm offered the following panegyric on the work: "Suffice it to say that it has long since been accepted as a crowning achievement of Ives's compositional career, and as one of the handful of works of pure genius written for the piano in the present century."[47]

Despite some lingering negative responses to Ives's stylistic heterogeneity, his pervasive use of borrowed materials, and his often-bewildering eclecticism, by the mid-1970s Ives's stature as "America's greatest composer" and Gilman's 1939 proclamation of the *Concord Sonata* as "the greatest music composed by an American" were gaining widespread acceptance.[48] Matching the critical attention in popular and scholarly circles, recordings of the *Concord Sonata* began to appear with exponential frequency. From 1948 to 1962 Kirkpatrick's 78 rpm (and later his long-playing reissue) was the only commercial recording available. Four recordings were added to the *Concord Sonata* discography in the 1960s, two released in 1962 (George Pappastavrou and Aloys Kontarsky) and two in 1968, including Kirkpatrick's second and Alan

Mandel's historic package of the complete piano music. Another four recordings appeared in the 1970s and at least eight were released in the 1980s and 1990s. Although all of these, including Kirkpatrick's to a lesser extent, use the second edition as their principal source, several pianists borrow elements from the first edition or other manuscript sources.

The performances on these recordings vary enormously in matters ranging from tempo to overall stylistic approach. Gilbert Kalish's 1977 recording is slow and meticulous (49 min., 23 sec.), Pappastavrou emphasizes Ives's lyricism, Kontarsky plays the work with often ferocious percussiveness and speed. The fastest and most mercurial of these recordings, not unlike the way Kirkpatrick remembered Ives's own playing in the late 1930s, "a deft, flitting kind of playing, often seeming to be all over the keyboard all at once," are, not surprisingly, Kirkpatrick's own (in 1968 Kirkpatrick clocked in at 37 min., 57 sec.).[49]

Fortunately, Ives, albeit past his prime, recorded two significant portions of "Emerson" and the complete "Alcotts" in 1943 (April 24), two years before Kirkpatrick's first recording and four years before the publication of the second edition. Although Ives took some liberties in tempo and exhibited such unnotated idiosyncrasies as playing the second note of a tie, more often the composer followed his score (the *second* edition) closely, if not slavishly. These excerpts also demonstrate Thomas M. Brodhead's assertion that "Ives desired a performance of any version of the 'Emerson' material to sacrifice tempo and rhythm in order to play the 'right notes' in difficult passages."[50]

Ives's Fourth Violin Sonata was introduced in the 1940s by the acclaimed Hungarian virtuoso Joseph Szigeti and the orchestral music has had powerful advocacy from prestigious conductors ranging from Leonard Bernstein in the 1950s to Michael Tilson-Thomas, Neeme Järvi, and Christoph von Dohnányi from the 1970s to the present. The songs have been recorded by such prominent opera and song recitalists as Thomas Stewart and Evelyn Lear, Jan DeGaetani, Roberta Alexander, and Dietrich Fischer-Dieskau. The situation with Ives's piano music is somewhat different. Many fine and acclaimed pianists have recorded the *Concord Sonata*, including Kalish (1977), Marc-André Hamelin (1990), and Easley Blackwood (1992).[51] Nevertheless, several generations of conservatory-trained and competition-circuit piano virtuosos since World War II – the pianists most heavily marketed and consequently most familiar to concert-goers and record collectors – have for the most part ignored the work.[52]

Thus, despite all the recognition and prestige, Ives's *Concord Sonata* remains, like other difficult modern works in various fields, more studied than read, seen, or, in this case, heard and played. At the turn of a new century the *Concord Sonata* is paying the price of canonization shared by other twentieth-century masterpieces. For some, the sonata remains too complex, too stylistically jarring, too long, and consequently too unpopular for conspicuous display and performance in our cultural institutions. Nevertheless, in addition to the proliferation of new recordings, the work continues to gain new friends and vigorous champions. In the not-too-distant future devotees may witness Ives's *Concord Sonata*, a work of certifiable historical importance and critical stature, joining compositions like the Liszt Sonata and perhaps even Beethoven's "Hammerklavier" in the obligatory repertoire of piano virtuosos.

3

Genesis

Ives's chronology

In a "memo" probably entered in 1933 Ives offered his most extended explanation of the *Concord Sonata* sources and their chronology (*Memos*, pp. 79–83). The time frame he presents at the outset of his remarks, "mostly between 1911 and 1915 (when it was finished)," agrees with the dates he offers on the final amended list of works he compiled about 1949 (*Memos*, pp. 79 and 162). In the 1933 memo Ives also cites specific completion dates for "Hawthorne" (October 12, 1911), "The Alcotts" (1913), and "Thoreau" (1915) (*Memos*, pp. 81–82).

Two years later in a written response to John Kirkpatrick's questions, Ives offers a specific completion date for "Emerson" ("summer of 1912"), a revised year for "The Alcotts" (1915), and confirms the dates offered in 1933 for "Hawthorne" and "Thoreau" (*Memos*, p. 202).[1] In a "second sketch" for this letter, Ives drafted, but did not send, the following recollection: "Shortly after 1911, at Pell's, I got the idea of a Concord sonata." Also in this letter Ives gives a 1919 date for his *Essays Before a Sonata*, a 1911 date for the *Emerson Overture* (presumably the "uncompleted score for orchestra" upon which the *Four Transcriptions from "Emerson"* were based), and assigns a time frame for the first transcription "sometime after 1915 and before 1918."

According to Ives's account, several works, nearly all eventually abandoned, featured material that would find their way into the *Concord Sonata* after 1911. One of these was an "Alcott Overture, 1904, with a theme and some passages used in the sonata" (*Memos*, p. 163). The earliest date Ives offered for future *Concord Sonata* material, April 1902, was intended for one such passage, which Ives recalled recycling in the "middle part" of "The Alcotts" (consonant and tonal in marked contrast to the sonata's dissonant and atonal norms) (*Memos*, p. 64, n. 2). Also in the 1933 memo Ives reveals that two passages in "Thoreau" were taken from a string quartet slow movement of 1905, "never finished or kept except this part" (*Memos*, p. 82).[2]

The composer recalled later in life that he had begun a piano concerto in 1907, the *Emerson Concerto*, which would, over the next four years, become inextricably intertwined with the *Emerson Overture*, like the earlier-conceived *Alcott Overture* one of several overtures based on literary figures (*Memos*, pp. 76 and 163).[3] In fact, the *Emerson Overture*, which features the piano prominently, and the *Emerson Concerto* may be the same work.[4] Music from the *Emerson Overture*, which Ives, perhaps not coincidentally, apparently abandoned as an independent work the year he first had "the idea of a Concord sonata" in 1911, also found its way into two studies, *Study No. 2* and *Study No. 9* (the latter more widely known as *The Anti-Abolitionist Riots*), as well as the "Emerson" movement of the *Concord Sonata* by 1914, the *Four Transcriptions from "Emerson"* by 1926, and the second edition of the *Concord Sonata* published in 1947.

Also according to his later recollections, in September 1910, one year before the *Concord Sonata* began to take shape as an independent work, Ives used future "Hawthorne" material as a starting point for the second movement of the Fourth Symphony. Although this movement would eventually follow *The Celestial Railroad* more closely than "Hawthorne," the solo piano part in the symphony would retain many direct musical connections with the earlier solo sonata piano movement. Originally planned as a movement for the Fourth Symphony in 1910, along with material derived "from themes in the unfinished Alcott overture, 1904," by 1911 the second movement of the Fourth Symphony and the "Hawthorne" movement of the *Concord Sonata* emerged as two related but separate works based on occasionally complementary material (*Memos*, pp. 64–65). In Ives's retelling, once he had conceived a *Concord Sonata* in 1911, he rapidly completed the two most complex movements, "Emerson" and "Hawthorne," by the following summer and had drafted enough of "The Alcotts" and "Thoreau" to be able to perform the "whole sonata" for his former Yale classmate and professional music critic Max Smith, also in 1912.

Debate over the chronology of Ives's music and especially the extent of his subsequent revisions has intensified since the late 1920s when Elliott Carter "got the impression that he [Ives] might have frequently jacked up the level of dissonance of many works as his tastes changed."[5] Even Ives authority and advocate John Kirkpatrick voiced doubts about a number of Ives's dates.[6] For this reason the above chronological summary gleaned from Ives's own recollections should not go unchallenged. Unfortunately, what is at stake in this debate is not only Ives's memory and his alleged priority as a modern composer but his personal integrity. We have heard from the accused. Now for the cross-examination.

Ives's chronology cross-examined

In 1987 Maynard Solomon, a widely respected music historian and psychiatrist who had written thought-provoking psychological studies of Beethoven, issued a challenge that Ives studies verify the composer's questionable chronology using methods developed for dating the manuscripts of Bach, Mozart, and Beethoven sketches, autograph scores, and other documentary materials.[7] Most provocatively, Solomon interpreted the inconsistencies in Ives's composition lists and habit of entering addresses and dates retrospectively as a "systematic pattern of falsification."[8] Solomon's interpretation has prompted considerable attention from the media at large as well as from Ives scholars. Included among the latter are thoughtful responses from J. Peter Burkholder, Philip Lambert, Carol Baron, Stuart Feder, and Gayle Sherwood. Solomon's questioning of Ives's motives and his challenge to Ives's "veracity" have proven particularly troubling and have become the principal point of agreement or refutation.

In a 1988 panel discussion devoted to the issues raised in Solomon's essay, Burkholder welcomed a thorough review of Ives's manuscripts but did "not think that the essential chronology of Ives's life and works is going to change a great deal."[9] Taking the lead from Ives editors Wayne Shirley and James Sinclair, Burkholder also indirectly challenges Solomon's implication that Ives's practice of revising compositions somehow diminishes his stature as a modern composer, since "the essential conception of a piece is usually its most radical aspect and almost always present from the first sketch."[10] While acknowledging Ives's practice of revising and altering scores, his inconsistency in dating them, and conceding that Ives "sometimes obscured facts," Lambert finds many of Solomon's conclusions to be equally "speculatively conceived."[11] In the absence of hard evidence, Lambert gives Ives rather than Solomon the benefit of a reasonable doubt.

In a 1990 essay Baron defended Ives's veracity after examining handwriting characteristics of three manuscripts with "verifiable performance dates" from three widely separate stages of Ives's compositional career: *The Celestial Country* (1902), the Third Violin Sonata (1914), and the revised full score of *Putnam's Camp* from *Three Places in New England* (1929).[12] Baron concluded that "with regard to dating *Putnam's Camp*, the entire short-score sketch was composed during the first half of the second decade of this century (not in 1920 or later, as had been claimed [by Solomon])." Baron also espoused the view that "many of the rhythmic innovations and the spikey dissonances" in the 1929 revisions of *Putnam's Camp* can be traced to *Country Band March* and *Overture and March 1776*, "which we can now date in the first decade of this century."[13]

In her attempt to minimize the significance of Ives's late addition of dissonances in *Putnam's Camp*, Baron also discusses the varying dissonant levels and their meanings in the first and second editions of "The Alcotts" (p. 54, sys. 1–2 in both editions). Baron writes: "Based on the fact that other left-hand octaves are filled in [with perfect or diminished fifths above the bass as in the second edition], this revision probably fulfils Ives's original intentions." What is remarkable about this conjectural observation is that, without apparently having consulted Ives's 1919 ink autograph score, Baron supports the documentary evidence that the filled-in octaves of the second edition were in fact identically "dissonanced" there.

The next major response to Solomon appeared in Stuart Feder's psycho-analytic biography, *Charles Ives: "My Father's Song"* (1992) in an appendix titled "On the Veracity of Ives's Dating of His Music."[14] Feder, like Solomon, also a psychiatrist, focuses on "Solomon's psychological formulation," which in Feder's view "is not so much wrong as incomplete" in that it "misses the complexity of motivation." While Feder considers the possibility that "Ives may well have been psychologically poised for retrospective falsification in the dating of his manuscripts," he concludes that the composer was constitutionally "incapable of the organized mental effort necessary for a systematic revision of his life's work." Feder notes that "Solomon's evidence is in itself circumstantial" and observes a disparity between Solomon's "vigorous assertions" and the tentative standing of his "working hypothesis." Although he quotes Kirkpatrick's conclusion that "all datings in Ives are problematical," Feder, in the light of Baron's preliminary refutation, decided to adopt Kirkpatrick's problematical but well-considered chronology rather than to accept "Solomon's musicological assertions" which "remain to be evaluated." According to Feder, Ives's "systematic pattern of falsification," like the Holy Roman Empire which was neither holy, Roman, nor an empire, was neither systematic, a pattern, nor demonstrably false.

The *Concord Sonata* is not one of the works under specific chronological contention in the 1987 essay, but in his 1989 point-counterpoint reply to Lambert's rebuttal Solomon does suggest that Ives's inconsistencies in dating this work might be consistent with a "systematic pattern of falsification."[15] Solomon is correct when he notes the absence of any documentary or even hearsay evidence that would substantiate Ives's claim to have performed his sonata in a New York church in 1914, but even a false or undocumented claim here does not, in itself, disprove Ives's other chronological recollections. Far more important to Ives's credibility is the veracity of his contemporary memo of 1913, where the composer discusses in some detail his performance of the *Concord Sonata* for Max Smith the previous year, and Smith's uncomprehending and largely unsympathetic response. Since the 1913 date can be plausibly determined from the unambiguous context of Ives's remarks, more evidence is needed to convict the composer of deliberately falsifying this document in the 1920s or '30s.[16] Here is the crucial passage:

> For instance, I played the whole sonata to Max Smith last year (1912) – the Hartsdale piano didn't help! – though the last, "Thoreau," in the middle section, I played partly from the sketch and with a few improvisations in a few places, as it was not all written out fully complete (but it was practically as it is now, though there are a few places I'll have to clean up). (*Memos*, p. 186)

This 1913 document appears as the first of three datable *Concord Sonata* memos. The second refers to letters received in 1921 and 1923

and is dated plausibly by Kirkpatrick "1923 or later," and Ives himself
dated the third memo "Jan. '29." Of particular relevance to the present
chronological argument is the fact that Ives wrote out a portion of the
second memo on the back flyleaves of a first edition copy.[17] Solomon suggests that Ives might be "retroactively drafting a diary entry to establish a
1912 performance date for the *Concord Sonata*," and he might have a case
if Ives had copied the *1913* memo in the 1920 edition flyleaves. Solomon
neglected to observe, however, that the entry in the *Concord Sonata* copy
was the second or *1923* memo and not the presumably more truthful first
memo of 1913.[18]

A revised genesis

The most detailed response to Solomon is Gayle Sherwood's Yale University dissertation on the chronology of Ives's choral works.[19] In contrast to Feder, who focuses on the psychological issues regarding Ives's
inconsistent datings, Sherwood accepts Solomon's challenge to "rely
upon the traditional methods of historical musicology – documentary
and paper studies, handwriting comparisons, and a detailed analytical
reconstruction of the compositional process of each work."[20] Following
the methods advocated by Solomon, Sherwood establishes the earliest
and latest dates (*terminus post* and *ante quem*) for every paper type that
Ives is known to have used.

Her extensive study of paper-type data combined with the fruits of
Baron's handwriting descriptions has enabled Sherwood to add seven
datable manuscripts to Baron's three. Sherwood's methods have led to
both confirmations and contradictions of Ives's retrospective chronology. Her study of the choral works and preliminary work on the songs
resulted in "a fine-tuning of Ives's and Kirkpatrick's dates" in the case of
the former and modest adjustments in the latter, while her tentative
initial exploration of the symphonies and violin sonatas suggests that
Ives's dates for some of these works are about five years premature.[21]

When added to Kirkpatrick's helpful and generally reliable *Catalogue*
identification of paper types for each page, Sherwood's research reveals a
more complex *Concord Sonata* chronology than previously thought. In
fact, the paper types that correspond with extant relevant datable manuscripts prior to the engraving of the first edition in late 1919 and 1920 fall

into *two* disparate and discrete periods, the first between 1907 and 1914 and the second from about 1915 to 1921. The first chronological phase, which is compatible with the time period outlined in Ives's chronology (1911–15), includes the largest extant portion, eight pages, of the *Emerson Overture* (f0565 and f2212–f2218), a brief sketch (labeled a "patch" by Kirkpatrick) for "Emerson" (f3911), and a few sketch pages for "Hawthorne," "The Alcotts," and "Thoreau" (f3955–f3956, and f3993).[22]

The handwriting on these earliest paper types is closer to 1914 than to 1907, two or three years later than Ives's stated completion dates for "Hawthorne" (1911) and "Emerson" (1912), and two years later than the "Thoreau" sketches Ives might have used when he performed this movement for Max Smith in 1912. A two- or three-year discrepancy between paper and handwriting might be explained, however, by the necessary limitations of the latter technique. It should also be noted that although Sherwood's data base of ten works provides a useful chronological yardstick for placing handwriting characteristics, the distance between 1907 and 1914 is still great and does not allow either for incremental changes or a precise demarcation where Ives entered a new handwriting phase. While the handwriting characteristics in Ives's *Concord Sonata* sketches may be closer to the Third Violin Sonata of 1914 than to the songs, *Spring Song* and *World's Highway* of 1907, it remains a fair question to ask how accurately a manuscript can be dated two or three years prior to the next handwriting phase.

The largest portion of the *Concord Sonata* sketch material was drafted on paper types, conveniently narrow in provenance, *which could not have been used prior to 1915*. This includes virtually all of the extant "Emerson" sketches (f3900–f3916), several pages now probably mistakenly included among the *Emerson Overture* papers (f2225 and f2227–f2228), and the ink autograph copies of all four movements. If Ives had in fact completed "Emerson" and "Hawthorne" and had begun to sketch "The Alcotts" and "Thoreau" by 1912, the physical remnants of this compositional process remain incomplete beyond the *Emerson Overture* drafts from 1914 or earlier (these manuscripts correspond to pages 1–5 and 18–19 of "Emerson" in the second published edition) as well as isolated sketches of the other movements. Included among the latter are two drafts of theme 1 (Appendix 1) the central "human faith melody" (f3252 and f3993). Both of these drafts, in contrast to its final form, lack the Beethoven's Fifth Symphony motive.

All that is absent from Ives's ink autograph score among the later extant "Emerson" sketches (some of this overlaps with the *Emerson Overture* sketches, but most of it is new), is musical material that would eventually appear in the published edition in "Emerson" (on pages 2–3 and 7). In contrast to the *Emerson Overture* sketches which exhibit handwriting characteristics compatible with Ives's chronology, the handwriting on these "Emerson" sketches (most notably those with music later found on pages 5–6, 8–11, and 13–17), places these pages on unidentified paper types between 1914 and 1919, "closer to 1919" in Sherwood's view. Other "Emerson" sketches on datable paper from 1915 to 1918 would serve Ives on his 1919 ink autograph score with material that corresponds to pages 12–13 and 17–18 of the second edition. Perhaps significantly, with a few isolated exceptions these later sketches contain music that does *not* appear among the extant sketches for the *Emerson Overture*.

The manuscript legacy outlined above does not contradict Ives's recollection that he had abandoned the *Emerson Overture* by 1911 or that he worked out a significant portion of a playable version of "Emerson," or at least its first pages, by 1912. Similarly, the manuscript evidence on the extant sketch pages of "Hawthorne," "The Alcotts," and "Thoreau" is compatible with Ives's timetable. Most of the "Emerson" sketches, however, including the relatively self-contained "verse" passsage from pages 8–11, first materialized *after* 1914 and perhaps as late as 1919. The paper trail thus points to considerable revision and probable expansion after Ives played a version of his sonata for Max Smith in 1912. The sketches do not yet reveal, however, whether Ives worked on the sonata sporadically between 1914 and 1918 or whether he returned to it closer to the time he prepared his autograph score, reliably placed before the autumn of 1919.

The two Concords

After distributing the first edition in 1921, Ives began to recast the *Concord Sonata* into new forms. The *Four Transcriptions from "Emerson"* (*c.* 1926), especially the first, combine elements of the abandoned

Emerson Overture and the "Emerson" movement into a new hybrid.[23] *The Celestial Railroad* (also *c.* 1926), more loosely derived from the "Hawthorne" movement and the original second movement of the Fourth Symphony, served, as persuasively argued by Thomas M. Brodhead, as the principal source of a revised second movement of Ives's Fourth Symphony.[24] Ives would also use seventeen copies of the engraved first edition (R^1–R^{17}) as a workshop for correcting details and exploring new possibilities. The revised first edition copy R^7 or Copy "A" (formerly numbered R^3) seems to exhibit a rudimentary planning stage for the *Transcriptions* and therefore antedates these compositional *Concord Sonata* byproducts by anywhere from one to five years. The revised copies bring together elements of the *Emerson Overture* in "Emerson," incorporate some material from *The Celestial Railroad* in "Hawthorne," and combine features of both the first and second editions in all the movements of the *Concord Sonata*.[25]

Although Ives continued to make minor revisions until the early 1940s, the completion of the *Four Transcriptions from "Emerson"* also completes the main compositional work on the second edition of the *Concord Sonata*. While Ives considered numerous variants on his revised first copies and second edition proofs, including some extended cuts and addenda in the former, in the end he chose not to incorporate the more "radical" departures beyond those retained from the *Transcriptions*. Even those *Transcription* revisions that Ives did adopt extend first edition material beyond a few beats on only two occasions.

Moreover, whether they restore previously discarded material from the *Emerson Overture* or from the 1919 ink autograph manuscript of the *Concord Sonata*, Ives's revisions between 1921 and 1926 (or later) do not alter either the structure or the overall dissonance level of the first edition. Several revision types can be readily distinguished: (1) restorations and rejections of earlier ideas derived from the *Emerson Overture* (*c.* 1907–14) and the 1919 ink autograph score of the sonata; (2) performance directions, including notational changes and additions that offer more precise ways to depict rhythm, directions on tempo, dynamics, accent marks, and hand positions; (3) corrections of first edition errors; and (4) the adoption of material (some of which may be new) from revised first-edition copy R^{15} and the seven subsequent sets of second edition proofs.[26]

Several changes in the second 1947 edition reflect Ives's evolving attitudes about whether to add or highlight, obscure or remove statements of key motives, including the opening four notes of Beethoven's Fifth Symphony. The manuscripts show that two prominent second edition statements of Beethoven's motive, abandoned in the first edition, were present in the *Emerson Overture* material or in the 1919 ink autograph score.[27] Ives had worked out another pair of revised treatments of Beethoven on revised first edition copies and *"Emerson" Transcription* sources before 1926.

In the first edition Ives included eight performance notes directly in the score. Those intended for specific passages are marked by an asterisk.[28] For the second edition Ives more than quadrupled this total and placed most of them as endnotes. Some of the thirty-four second edition notes address specific technical suggestions to help pianists negotiate difficult passages or alternatives (especially in "Hawthorne") and to maintain the speed of a difficult passage.[29] Others add programmatic asides not included in the *Essays* (see chapter 6).[30]

In addition to the many new performance notes in the back of the second edition that can be connected with an asterisk (or star) in the main score, another thirteen asterisks are lacking a note. Fortunately, these unpublished performance notes can be found among Ives's Literary Writings in the Ives Collection at Yale University (Series II, A).[31] Four of the unpublished notes refer to passages in the score not marked by an asterisk.[32]

By way of summary, the following points encapsulate what is known about the complex genesis of the *Concord Sonata*:

1) Ives apparently evolved the idea of a *Concord Sonata* by stages, starting with overtures based on individual literary figures as early as 1904 and perhaps even 1902 (early discernible traces appear no later than *c.* 1907–08).

2) Around 1911 (according to him) Ives conceived the sonata as a concept – this date seems supported by his ceasing work on portions of the *Emerson Concerto* about this time.

3) In 1912 (according to him) Ives played a version of the *Concord Sonata* for Max Smith – some of this version may have been played from rudimentary sketches or worked out in Ives's fingers.

4) In 1915 or later the real work of composition is evident in the datable sketch materials – apparently much of this work was done in 1919.[33]

5) Even if Ives did not produce a complete work similar to what became known as the first edition until several years after 1915, this version was certainly composed no later than the autumn of 1919 (when the engraving process began).

6) Between *c.* 1921–26 Ives returned to the *Emerson Overture* and to discarded material in the 1919 ink autograph score, the first and most decisive stages towards a new edition of the *Concord Sonata*.

7) Based largely on the *Emerson Overture*, the ink autograph score, the *Four Transcriptions from "Emerson," The Celestial Railroad*, considerable tinkering on seventeen first edition copies, and seven sets of proofs the second edition of the *Concord Sonata* appeared in 1947 – in addition to the restorations and rejection of earlier ideas, the principal revisions in the second edition are changes and additions in notation, corrections of earlier errors, and many new explanatory performance notes for specific passages.[34]

4

Form and design

Like other modernists, Ives endeavored to create an idiosyncratic and compelling musical response to the competing aesthetic and technical principles that marked the end of the nineteenth century and the early decades of the twentieth. Thus, despite such prominent signs of modernism as pervasive atonality and dissonant counterpoint, Ives's *Concord Sonata* might also be viewed as a continuation rather than a retreat from the musical ideals of an earlier era. Just as Beethoven had explored the boundaries of classical sonata form and style without abandoning its fundamental ideologies, so Ives stretched and reinterpreted the nineteenth-century European and American traditions.

Although Ives called his *Concord Sonata* and other multi-movement works for piano (or violin and piano) a sonata "for want of a more exact name," a common thread of techniques among the works so designated reveals that Ives did, in fact, distinguish between sonatas, "sets," and other descriptive experimental works with or without programmatic titles.[1] For Ives, as for other nineteenth-century composers who followed in Beethoven's wake, the appellation "sonata" meant a substantial and usually serious-minded multi-movement or multi-sectional composition in a tradition that could accommodate works as different as Liszt's B minor Piano Sonata or the formally more conservative chamber sonatas of Brahms.

In common with other historically important compositions, including non-sonatas such as Schubert's *Wanderer Fantasy* for piano and the operas of Wagner, works that Ives chose to designate as sonatas borrowed freely from the ubiquitous nineteenth-century techniques of cyclic form, thematic transformation, and the development of motivic families. Less typically for an extended piano work, Ives's *Concord Sonata* also contains considerable programmatic content. Programmatic works, more common in symphonies, tone poems, and overtures and orchestral interludes from operas, entered the mainstream of nineteenth-century European tradition as early as Beethoven's Sixth Symphony (*Pastoral*), first performed in 1808, and retained their currency between Berlioz's *Symphonie fantastique* (1830) and Dvořák's *New World Symphony* (1893). While the borrowing of pre-existent thematic material was less usual (or more circumspect), it will be noted in chapter 5 that borrowing grew increasingly prevalent in the late-nineteenth century (the decades before Ives attained his early maturity), in America as well as Europe.

Motivic fabric

Just as a synopsis of most plays benefits from the introduction of at least the major characters, a synopsis of Ives's *Concord Sonata* will be greatly facilitated by a playbill of its themes and motives. Appendix 1, "*Concord Sonata* themes," is designed to provide this reference tool while Appendix 2, "Formal and thematic outline," will show where these themes and motives fall within the overall form of the work (see pp. 80–86). The *Concord Sonata*, like Wagner's *Ring* and other large-scale nineteenth-century music, programmatic and non-programmatic alike, includes a vast and labyrinthine network of thematic fragments (and their rhythmic and melodic transformations), miscellaneous original and borrowed themes, thematic reminiscences, and foreshadowings of Ives's own past and future compositions. Two musically and programmatically interrelated thematic families, however, emerge as centrally prominent (albeit in varying degrees), from one movement to another. They will be referred to in this handbook as the "human faith" family and the "corn field" family. The families are illustrated in Examples 4.1 and 4.2. Other important non-cyclical themes and motives, original and borrowed, figure prominently. Some of these relate tangentially either motivically or programmatically to one or both of the two principal families. They also share the fate of themes in more traditional "classical" sonata developments and are worked out, sometimes exhaustively, in individual movements.

Most of the "human faith melody" (theme 1), a designation Ives himself used in his essay on "The Alcotts," is based on a series of seven connected motivic fragments that range in length from three to eight

Ex. 4.1 "Human faith" family

a "human faith melody," p. 57, sys. 4–5 (App. 1, 1)

b main "Emerson" lyric theme, p. 5, sys. 1 (see Ex. 4.2 c below)

Slowly and quietly

c Beethoven, Fifth Symphony (App. 1, 7)

d *Martyn* (App. 1, 8)

e *Missionary Chant* (App. 1, 4)

Ex. 4.1 (*continued*)

f Beethoven, "Hammerklavier" Sonata (App. 1, 9)

g "Columbia, the Gem of the Ocean" (App. 1, 10; see Ex. 4.2 e below)

notes (see Ex. 4.1 a). Each fragment can be interpreted either as a quotation or an allusion to borrowed or original themes that Ives will develop separately in the course of the work. Examples 4.3 and 4.4 show the most extended "human faith melody" statements in "Emerson" and "Hawthorne." Most, but significantly not all, of the long "human faith melody" is heard somewhat obscurely but relatively early in "Emerson" (p. 2, sys. 2–3, illustrated in Ex. 4.3 a), and most of the second half of this central theme is heard three times at "Emersons"'s close (p. 18, sys. 5 and p. 19, sys. 2–4, the first of these is illustrated in Ex. 4.3 b). After one well-developed section on pages 30–32 and numerous shorter references in "Hawthorne" (the extended passage is shown in Ex. 4.4), the motives coalesce into a complete and connected melody twice in "The Alcotts" on pages 55 and 57 (the second of these is shown in Ex. 4.1 a). Finally, in "Thoreau" Ives presents the "human faith melody" in the flute part on the last two pages of the sonata. On this valedictory occasion only the final note is missing.

The "corn field" family (Ex. 4.2 a–f) is so-called because its members relate in some identifiable familial way to the "Down in the Corn Field" refrain of Stephen Foster's "Massa's in De Cold Ground" (Appendix 1, theme 18). After considerable foreshadowing in the first three movements, Foster's motive is eventually introduced and prominently displayed in "Thoreau." The "corn field" family is comprised of a series of five distinct and varied five-note descending scales (and one four-note variant). The mostly lyrical "corn field" family members appear in both

Ex. 4.2 "Corn field" family

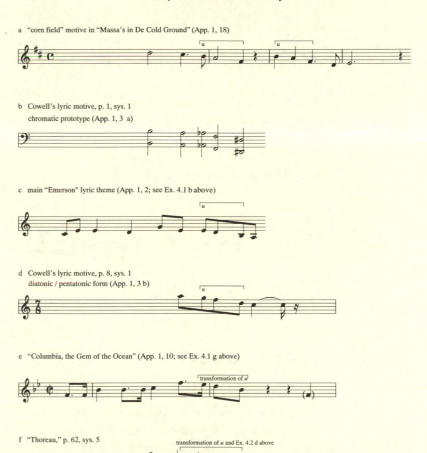

a "corn field" motive in "Massa's in De Cold Ground" (App. 1, 18)

b Cowell's lyric motive, p. 1, sys. 1
chromatic prototype (App. 1, 3 a)

c main "Emerson" lyric theme (App. 1, 2; see Ex. 4.1 b above)

d Cowell's lyric motive, p. 8, sys. 1
diatonic / pentatonic form (App. 1, 3 b)

e "Columbia, the Gem of the Ocean" (App. 1, 10; see Ex. 4.1 g above)

f "Thoreau," p. 62, sys. 5

chromatic and diatonic/pentatonic versions and in various states of recognizability from the first page to the last.

Even a cursory glance at Examples 4.1 and 4.2 reveals considerable intermarriage between the offspring of the two principal motivic families. A three-note motive that is frequently, often prominently, displayed throughout the sonata, but especially in "Emerson" and "Hawthorne," links the two families most directly. This motive, which consists of a

Ex. 4.3 "Human faith melody" in "Emerson"

a "Emerson," p. 2, sys. 2–3

b "Emerson," p. 18, sys. 5

Ex. 4.4 "Human faith melody" in "Hawthorne"

p. 30, sys. 3 – p. 32, sys. 4

descending major second followed by a descending minor third, introduced as motive *u* in Ex. 4.1 a, will eventually "grow" into the "corn
field" theme (cf. Ex. 4.1 b and Ex. 4.2 a, c, and d). Both families also share
distinctive fragments of Simeon B. Marsh's hymn *Martyn* (Appendix 1,
theme 8) and David T. Shaw's patriotic song, "Columbia, the Gem of the
Ocean" (Appendix 1, theme 10). The connections among these fragments are also shown in Examples 4.1 and 4.2.

Although it does not do justice to the extensive and intricate fabric of
themes that Ives weaves, Examples 4.5, 4.6, and 4.7 partially illustrate
the journey of two Ives motives (the opening four-note incipits of
Beethoven's Fifth Symphony and Ives's "human faith melody") and the
fugue subject that may be based on Wagner's *Prelude* to *Tristan und
Isolde*. With the exception of "Thoreau," which emphasizes the "corn

field" family and delays the "human faith melody" until its final two pages, Beethoven's Fifth Symphony motive (Ex. 4.1 c) is the most ubiquitously heard in the sonata, either with the major or minor descending third intervals of Beethoven's initial two statements. The connections between the two principal borrowed hymns, *Martyn* (theme 8) and Charles Zeuner's *Missionary Chant* (theme 14), and Beethoven's famous motive have long been noticed (see Ex. 4.1 c–e). On numerous occasions Ives alters the final note to something other than a descending minor or major third, for example, the ascending minor third and the descending augmented fourth sounding successively on page 18 (Ex. 4.5 d). Other times Ives abandons Beethoven's pitches entirely while preserving his rhythm, calling attention to it through vigorous accents (Ex. 4.5 e).

Also readily perceived is the connection between Beethoven's short-short-short-long rhythm and the first four notes of the "human faith melody," runner-up to Beethoven in frequency (introduced in Ex. 4.6 a). These four notes, too, recur in different guises. The most frequent alteration occurs with the fourth note. Instead of falling a perfect fifth, on a number of occasions this final note will ascend a perfect fourth; less frequently, Ives offers a more radical departing final interval such as descending augmented sixth (see Ex. 4.6 c–d).

The most frequent form of the *Tristan* motive, based on the opening six notes of Wagner's famous *Prelude* to *Tristan und Isolde* (Appendix 1, theme 11), makes its exclusive appearance in "Emerson" (see Ex. 4.7 a). After its introduction at the end of the second system in counterpoint with the first four notes of the main "Emerson" lyric theme, a combination that will occur often in the future (Ex. 4.7 b, also shown in Ex. 4.8), the *Tristan* motive returns in section 2 with one four-note and two six-note successive statements on page 5, systems 3–4. At the end of page 5 Ives introduces a hybrid motive in which the opening of the main "Emerson" lyric theme (now beginning with a minor rather than its usual major third) elides with the three-note chromatic descent characterisic of the *Tristan* motive (Ex. 4.7 c).

After disappearing in sections 3 and 4, Ives's *Tristan* motive appears repeatedly and prominently in sections 5–7. In the penultimate measure of section 5 (m. 8) Ives also introduces an inverted form of the motive (Ex. 4.7 d), a transformation which will return several times in section 6 and once in section 7. Having planted the idea of starting the motive with

Ex. 4.5 Beethoven's Fifth Symphony in "Emerson"

a   Beethoven Fifth Symphony (App. 1, 7)

b   "Emerson," p. 18, sys. 1

c   "Emerson," p. 12, sys. 2

d   "Emerson," p. 18, sys. 2

e   "Emerson," p. 6, sys. 1

Ex. 4.6 "Human faith melody," the first four notes

a "Emerson" (p. 1, sys. 1)

b "Hawthorne" (p. 21, sys. 3–4)

c "Hawthorne" (p. 28, sys. 2)

d "Hawthorne" (p. 30, sys. 3)

an ascending interval other than a diminished fifth in Ex. 4.7 c (in this case a minor third), in section 5 (m. 6) Ives tantalizingly suggests the correct Wagnerian incipit with its opening ascending minor sixth. Nevertheless, at the same time he obfuscates Wagner's interval by inserting an intervening note to form a minor seventh (Ex. 4.7 e).

Tristan appears sometimes as a four-note motive but mainly as a six-note motive, or its inversion, the former usually and the latter invariably opening with a diminished fifth. On two occasions in "Emerson" (the opening of section 5, p. 13, sys. 4–5 and section 7, p. 17, sys. 2), however,

Ex. 4.7 *Tristan* motive and fugue subject in "Emerson"

a Wagner, *Prelude* to *Tristan und Isolde* (App. 1, 11)

b first appearance, with first four notes of main "Emerson" lyric theme, p. 1, sys. 2–3

c main "Emerson" lyric theme (App. 1, 2; see Exs. 4.1 b and 4.2 c above)

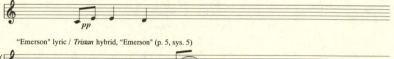

"Emerson" lyric / *Tristan* hybrid, "Emerson" (p. 5, sys. 5)

d "Emerson," p. 14, sys. 1

e *Tristan* motive transformed (first four notes), p. 13, sys. 5, m. 3

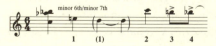

f *Tristan* fugue subject (thirteen notes), p. 13, sys. 4, mm. 1–2

Ives expands the *Tristan* motive into an extended thirteen-note fugue subject with matching rhythms as shown in Ex. 4.7 f.[2] In section 5 Ives even follows the subject (mm. 1–3) with two only slightly altered eleven-note answers at the fifth (mm. 4–7).

Tonal characteristics

Although Ives does not harmonize his melodies using traditional functional tonality, he does highlight certain pitches as harmonically significant and tonally suggestive. As Arthur Berger wrote of Stravinsky's "pre-twelve-tone" compositions, "there are other means besides functional ones for asserting pitch-class priority."[3] An analogous non-functional tonality pervades much of the *Concord Sonata*. The mostly atonal "Emerson" movement nonetheless emphasizes a sense of C in its statements of the main "Emerson" lyric theme that introduces sections 2 and 6 (Appendix 1, theme 2), the C pedals in the bass and point of melodic arrival at the end of each phrase in most of section 3, and the boisterous C minor statements on pages 6 and 13. In its final section (pp. 18–19) various tonalities are implied to accompany Beethoven's transposed Fifth Symphony and "Hammerklavier" motives in upper and inner voices, including G major, F major, A major, E-flat major (two times), and finally (despite some ambiguity) in the bass, F major, to end the movement.

Traditional four-part harmony briefly surfaces in "Hawthorne," first with the strongly tonal chords in G major (tonic, dominant, and supertonic on p. 33), followed at greater length with the F-sharp harmonization of *Martyn* on page 34. The *Country Band March* self-borrowing that follows on page 35 strongly suggests A-flat major before it moves into less tonal territory after four measures. The rag on page 38 is strikingly bitonal (C and E-flat major), and the opening of "The Alcotts" combines B-flat and A-flat.[4] After concluding the first section with the "human faith melody" in B-flat major (p. 55, sys. 2–3), most of the middle section of "The Alcotts" (pp. 55–56) faithfully adheres to E-flat major (beginning on p. 55, sys. 3, m. 2); the second statement of the "human faith melody" concludes this movement with a firm affirmation of the C that had haunted so much of "Emerson" (Ex. 4.1 a). In "Thoreau" Ives's occasional highlighting of the subdominant and dominant (G and A) throughout much of the movement eventually leads to a tonic D tonal center at its close. Bitonal elements surface here too, for example the opening and closing sequence of arpeggios (A and D-sharp major) and the procession of bitonal triads on page 65, system 2. The "human faith melody" itself on pages 67–68 hovers between B-flat major and G minor.[5]

Form

Formally, the *Concord Sonata* presents a taxonomic challenge. Ives suggested in his famous description that the work is "a group of four pieces, called a sonata for want of a more exact name" (*Essays*, xxv) and indeed, the *Concord Sonata* eschews the formal structure of classical sonata form. Nevertheless, it does preserve the nineteenth-century structural and aesthetic principles of cyclic form, thematic transformation, developing variation, and a philosophic and narrative programmaticism. Ives's characteristic atonal harmonic language and the high level of dissonant harmony and counterpoint, however, leave the worlds of both eighteenth- and nineteenth-century piano sonatas far behind and places his *Concord Sonata* more compatibly in the company of such modernist pre-World War I compositions by Schoenberg, Berg, and Stravinsky.

Ives's "impressionistic pictures of Emerson and Thoreau" are conveyed through a form that resembles a rondo perhaps more closely than any other classical form. In contrast to classical or romantic rondos, however, Ives's "rondo" themes never recur precisely in their original form (in fact, more typically they diverge radically from their source), nor do they adhere to classical formal boundaries. The "sketch of the Alcotts" corresponds roughly to an A-B-A' framework, but here too the second A' sounds more like a variation than a reprise of the first. "Hawthorne," formally the most enigmatic and inchoate, nonetheless can be conveniently, if not entirely neatly, arranged in three sections (each with two or three identifiable smaller subsections).[6]

The formal divisions outlined and encapsulated in Appendix 2 are for the most part clear. The murkier ones, especially in "Emerson" and "Thoreau," were sometimes selected to emphasize the "rondo" elements. Thus, returns of significant thematic material inaugurate a "new" section however brief, for example the nine measures of

"Emerson"'s section 5 and the relatively brief sections 3 and 5 in "Thoreau." Other possible choices, of course, might have deemphasized the rondo character of these movements.

Complementing these formal shapes are the so-called extra-musical features of the sonata. For example, the second large section of "Hawthorne" contains several certifiable programmatic elements, and much of the "Thoreau" movement fits Ives's program of Thoreau's "thought on an autumn day of Indian summer at Walden" (*Essays*, 67). The philosophical and programmatic content of all four movements will be addressed in chapter 6.

Within the first section of "Emerson" (the first four systems shown in Ex. 4.8 alone include themes 1, 2, 3 a–b, 4, 7–9, and 11 from Appendix 1) Ives has introduced all the *Concord Sonata* themes that will be transformed and eventually completed later in the movement.[7] Several of these themes will return in new forms in subsequent movements as well. Also in the first section Ives inaugurates the practice, especially prominent in "Emerson," of presenting duets and even trios of motives contrapuntally, for example, on the first page the "Emerson" motive (treble) against the first four notes of the "human faith melody" (sys. 2).[8]

Although the rest of the movement exhibits a variety of themes, motives, and combinations of themes and motives, each of the next six sections (sections 2–7) focuses primarily on one of the principal "Emerson" themes introduced in section 1. Sections 2, 6, and 7 start with and continue to emphasize either the whole or a portion of the main "Emerson" lyric theme (Appendix 1, theme 2, Ex. 4.1 b and Ex. 4.2 c). Sections 3 and 4 offer variations on this lyric theme's progeny, in particular the five-note diatonic form of Henry Cowell's lyric theme, theme 3b (Ex. 4.2 d). Section 3 presents an unmistakable theme and variations on Cowell's motive (T–V1–V2–V3–Episode–T'). The brief section 5 features the *Tristan* motive (theme 11) and its inversion as well as the extended *Tristan* fugue subject and answer (Ex. 4.7 a–f). The concluding section 8 emphasizes the two Beethoven references embedded in the "human faith melody," themes 7 and 9 (Ex. 4.1 c and f), and in the space of two pages manages to display no less than nine varied statements of the "Emerson" motive, theme 4.

For most of "Hawthorne" Ives leaves the characteristically reflective

Ex. 4.8 Opening of "Emerson," p. 1, sys. 1–4

world of "Emerson," especially its conclusion, far behind. In addition to the contrasts between these movements in tempo, style, and character are contrasts in approach to motivic exposition and development. Not only are motives in "Hawthorne" fewer and farther between, the motives themselves are typically fragmented and distorted, sometimes seemingly beyond recognition. His treatment of motive u, for example, transforms its character and soon its intervallic integrity, preserving its opening interval (major or minor second) but only the principle of a final descending interval. Also, in contrast to "Emerson," combinations of motives in "Hawthorne" are the exception rather than the rule. Further, beyond motive u from "Emerson" and the "Columbia" motive (both derived from the "human faith" family), Ives avoids the "corn field" family of motives entirely (see Ex. 4.2).

The "Emerson" and "Hawthorne" movements demonstrate the nearly ubiquitous presence of three fragments of the "human faith melody," Ex. 4.1 a, segments t, u, and x (the last of these is Beethoven's Fifth Symphony motive). Nevertheless, although most of the first half and all of the second half of the "human faith melody" have been heard in the first two movements, even the longest segments in "Emerson" and "Hawthorne" (Ex. 4.3 and Ex. 4.4) either omit one or more parts of this extended theme or fail to present the whole theme in a continuous manner without melodic, rhythmic, or contrapuntal interruptions and distortions. All this changes in "The Alcotts," which offers the briefest, least dissonant, and otherwise most conventional and accessible *Concord Sonata* movement. "The Alcotts" introduces the complete and definitive form of the "human faith melody" on no less than two occasions, the first in B-flat major to close the first section (p. 55, sys. 1–3) and in C major at the end of the movement (p. 57, sys. 4–5, shown in Ex. 4.1 a).[9]

Few passages in the first three movements do not incorporate at least some portion of the "human faith melody." In contrast, "Thoreau" emphasizes the "corn field" family and especially, for the first time in the sonata, the original form of Foster's motive for which the family is named. After some foreshadowing on the first page, "rondo" elements begin to emerge with the "corn field" motive dominating or leading sections 3, 6, and figuring prominently at the end of section 7. Sections 4 and 5 explore a new transformation of motive u, Ex. 4.2 f, also possibly derived from the "corn field" motive. Only on the penultimate page of the sonata does the "human faith melody" (the first portion of which was foreshadowed in section 4), return for a nearly complete and continuous statement in the flute (p. 67, sys. 1–p. 68, sys. 1).[10] Instead of the *Martyn*/"Columbia" hybrid figure that closed the two complete statements of the "human faith melody" in "The Alcotts" (segment z), however, Ives halts the return of Beethoven's motive in the flute after its first three notes. The piano part completes the major third (spelled as a diminished fourth) as a quiet overtone marked "*pppp*."

The Foster phrase which introduced the "corn field" motive at the beginning of section 6 in "Thoreau" (p. 65, sys. 3, after the fermata), also introduces as well as concludes a final statement of this motive, both in its original form and its transformation. Ingeniously, Ives links the "corn field" motive with the "human faith melody" through the insistent A-C-G ostinato that began on the last system of page 67. As previously noted, in the final system of the sonata, Ives uses the ostinato arpeggio as the starting point for a return to the bitonal arpeggio that opened the movement (A and D-sharp). On the last beats Ives states Beethoven's Fifth Symphony rhythm on a static and hollow incomplete chord A-D-A with changing inner voices that tend to make the chord's possible dominant function somewhat ambiguous. Supporting Beethoven's rhythm is a sustained G, a prolongation of the seventh from the previous continuously moving A-C-G ostinato. By the time the major third (C-sharp) appears as the last new sound of the piece (a C-sharp had been foreshadowed with the A of the final ostinato several beats earlier), the harmonic support changes to D. The C-sharp can thus be heard as the leading tone of D, or at least a note that conveys a powerful sense of anticipation and irresolution. Henry Cowell's remarks on this final cadence still merit quotation:

> And never has the leading tone been fraught with so many implications. It will obviously resolve to the upper tonic eventually, and it now leads toward this point with yearning and intensity. But one is inescapably led to the realization that this suggestion of simultaneous tonic and dominant chords has only opened a new cycle of duality on a new plane of musico-philosophical existences. As the Sonata concludes, one senses that the ending is not final and that the music will continue to sound in the imagination and to grow.[11]

5

Borrowing

From blatant full-blown quotation to hidden allusions, the practice of musical borrowing constitutes a central feature of Ives's music. Since Ives borrowed in virtually all of his major compositions (mainly from hymns and popular music and to a lesser extent from European classical music), the subject is a vast one. Gradually a consensus has developed among scholars and critics that Ives carefully selected his borrowings for their common musical or programmatic denominators and that he exploited these shared characteristics with considerable skill and craft.[1]

Ives perhaps borrowed more extensively and in more varied ways than earlier composers, but he was certainly not the first extensive musical borrower. In fact, Ives's predecessors both in Europe and America borrowed classical and folk music material or modeled their compositions on earlier masters far more than they ackowledged in public or private statements.[2]

Beginning in the early 1980s the work of J. Peter Burkholder has cast considerable light on the range and complexity of Ives's borrowing as well as its diverse contexts and meanings.[3] In the process Burkholder has demonstrated the limitations of the all–purpose designation "quotation." In its place he has identified and described a wide variety of borrowing types, ranging, in roughly chronological sequence, from such familiar procedures as theme and variation, modeling, and paraphrase to the less common (although not unprecedented) practice of cumulative setting and later by increasingly complex borrowing techniques including quodlibet and collage. Literal quotation beyond a few notes is relatively rare, and even in those movements which employ cumulative settings, the full melodic statements heard at the end of the movement might be paraphrased versions of their tunes rather than their quotation.

Burkholder has also shown that even when the borrowings are disguised beyond recognition, they usually lie at the compositional center rather than the periphery of a movement. In a cumulative setting, the most frequent type of borrowing in the sonatas and symphonic music of Ives's maturity, a tune will gradually emerge out of obscurity; thus its recognition occurs retrospectively. Characteristically, when he paraphrases a pre-existent tune, a recognizable phrase that seemingly appears without warning as a "quote" can be identified through observable "clues" in earlier more distant paraphrases. The cumulative process in the *Concord Sonata* departs from Ives's usual practice in two ways: first, the process is delayed for three movements (the cumulative theme is not heard completely and continuously until "The Alcotts," see Ex. 4.1 a), and second, the borrowed theme or "human faith melody" is itself comprised of pre-existing themes (most borrowed) rather than a central source.

A rigorous and comprehensive examination of Ives's musical career has led Burkholder to conclude that Ives selected and then worked out his borrowed material mainly for musical rather than programmatic reasons. Many borrowings are chosen generically within the programmatic context of music whose principal subject matter is the act of music making.[4] Other borrowings are chosen for symbolic rather than illustrative purposes. After Burkholder's persuasive arguments it will be a difficult challenge for future Ives scholars and critics to defend the view that Ives was a composer who masked a poverty of imagination by indiscriminate and capricious quoting.

The overall plan of this chapter is to trace historically the various attributions that have been made from Ives's own statements in 1920 to those newly presented in this handbook. It will also address the following questions. To what extent did Ives borrow in the *Concord Sonata*? How do we distinguish a borrowing from a coincidental resemblance? In what ways do Ives's borrowings depart from their original sources? The philosophical and programmatic meanings behind the borrowings will be addressed in chapter 6. For a comprehensive listing of borrowings, both unequivocal and speculative, readers should consult the table at the end of this chapter, "Musical borrowings in the *Concord Sonata*" (pp. 61-64).

Borrowings: Ives, Cowell, and Kirkpatrick

Ives himself acknowledged only two *Concord Sonata* borrowings by name, Beethoven's Fifth Symphony (Appendix 1, theme 7) and Foster's

"Massa's in De Cold Ground" (theme 18). The former attribution appears in his *Essays Before a Sonata* (1920), the latter in his notes to the second edition (1947).[5] Significantly, these two acknowledged themes are the only themes that generate a family of motives (see Exx. 4.1 and 4.2).[6] They are also perhaps the only two themes which convey unequivocal and certifiable programmatic and musical meaning in the sonata. Beethoven's Fifth Symphony is featured prominently "as itself" and in various transformations in every movement; Foster's tune appears as the last in a series of metamorphoses of motive *u* (derived from the "human faith melody") and only in "Thoreau" (see chapter 4).

Some additional borrowings not directly acknowledged, or referred to without specificity in the *Essays*, are nonetheless unmistakable, e.g., the hymns, Marsh's *Martyn* ("Jesus, lover of my soul") (Appendix 1, theme 8) and Zeuner's *Missionary Chant* ("Ye Christian heralds, go, proclaim") (theme 14), Shaw's patriotic song "Columbia, the Gem of the Ocean" (theme 10), and Ives's own *Country Band March*. Most of the remaining borrowings are debatable, ambiguous, or fail one or two of Allen Gimbel's useful criteria (usually points 2 or 4) for deciding whether a musical passage is a quotation. Gimbel's criteria are these: "(1) the pitch pattern corresponds to a preexisting pattern in the musical literature (rhythm need not reflect this correspondence); (2) the composer sets this pattern in relief; (3) it can be documented that the composer was familiar with the work or passage in question; (4) the extramusical context of the composer's work is reflected by that of the quoted work."[7] A number of the *Concord Sonata* borrowings are allusions or musical puns, and thereby excluded from Gimbel's standard. The self-borrowing and foreshadowings of Ives's own future compositional activity also fall outside the reach of Gimbel's criteria. The following remarks will survey the history of these attributions with Gimbel's applicable criteria in mind.

Before the team biography by Henry and Sidney Cowell, *Charles Ives and His Music* (1955), reviews and essays on the *Concord Sonata* rarely mention specific borrowings by name or even Ives's practice of borrowing. Among the various initial critical responses to the work's public debut in 1921 only the anonymous reviewer in the *Musical Courier* noted a possible borrowing when he observed that Ives "lifted" *Missionary Chant*, "consciously or unconsciously," adding the hypothesis that

Charles Zeuner "would be scandalized could he see his tune all undressed."[8] Writing in 1935 in an entry that perhaps marks Ives's first entry in a history of music, Theodore M. Finney, without naming names, stated that Ives "has quietly developed a style which depends somewhat on New England folk idioms."[9]

The proliferation of reviews and profiles generated by John Kirkpatrick's 1939 *Concord Sonata* premiere similarly avoided the issue of Ives's borrowing in the *Concord Sonata* and elsewhere. A notable exception is Elliott Carter's widely quoted indictment of the practice (along with a litany of other musical and ideological weaknesses).[10] Carter writes: "The esthetic is naive, often too naive to express serious thoughts, frequently depending on quotation of well-known American tunes, with little comment, possibly charming, but certainly trivial." It therefore comes as something of a surprise when in the next paragraph Carter mentions a "pilgrim's song" (without assigning a specific tune to it) along with "the funny parody of 'Hail! Columbia'" in "Hawthorne" (Clayton W. Henderson, *The Charles Ives Tunebook*, no. 77) as among the highlights of the work.[11] Although Ives knew "Hail! Columbia" and used it in several works, Carter is almost certainly confusing two songs that contain the word "Columbia" in their title. In any event, "Hail! Columbia" is an incorrect attribution.

The next writer to comment on Ives's borrowing is Henry Cowell in the "music" portion of *Charles Ives and His Music*.[12] In his essay on "The Alcotts" Ives refers to Beth Alcott, who "played the old Scotch airs, and played at the Fifth Symphony" (*Essays*, p. 47). Cowell specifies "Loch Lomond" (Appendix 1, theme 15) as one of these "Scotch airs" (Ex. 5.1 a), an attribution that will be abandoned, perhaps too cavalierly, by future lists of borrowings including Kirkpatrick's *Catalogue* and Henderson's *Tunebook*.[13] Such borrowed elements as the Scottish snaps in the middle portion of "The Alcotts" may be more generically Scottish rather than assignable to a specific tune. Nevertheless, both "Loch Lomond" and Ives's "Scotch air" share the recurring major second-minor third motive with its inverted descent ("on the bonnie, bonnie banks of Loch Lomond"). The five-note descending melodic line in "Loch Lomond" on "ever wont to be" also corresponds exactly with the melodic conclusion to Ives's tune. For these reasons this handbook will resurrect "Loch Lomond" as a borrowed tune. Cowell also noted that

Ex. 5.1 Three borrowings in "The Alcotts"

a "Loch Lomond" (App. 1, 15)

But me and my true love will nev-er meet a - gain, on the

b Wagner, *Wedding March* from *Lohengrin* (App. 1, 16)

Treu - lich ge - führt

c Winnemore, "Stop that Knocking at My Door" (App. 1, 17)

I once did__ lub a co-lord Gal__ Whose

"The Alcotts" (p. 55, sys. 3 – p. 56, sys. 1)

Slower and quietly

Ives follows both appearances of his "Scotch air" with the opening measure of Wagner's *Wedding March* from *Lohengrin* (Appendix 1, theme 16), widely known in Great Britain and North America as "Here comes the bride" (Ex. 5.1 b). Although the quotation is fragmentary and the programmatic meaning is unclear, Ives's rhythm and harmony as well as melody are identical to Wagner's famous march.

The next major source of Ives's *Concord Sonata* borrowings is Kirkpatrick's *Catalogue*. Kirkpatrick vigorously denied the possibility that this resemblance to the *Wedding March* could be interpreted as anything more than a coincidence.[14] He also omitted Cowell's "Loch Lomond" attribution from the short list of unequivocal "Alcotts" borrowings in his *Catalogue* (Beethoven's Fifth Symphony and Zeuner's *Missionary Chant*). Kirkpatrick does, however, offer three unmistakable "Hawthorne" borrowings not previously cited by Cowell or other earlier writers: *Martyn*, "Columbia, the Gem of the Ocean" (listed by Kirkpatrick as "The Red, White, and Blue"), and Ives's own *Country Band March* (Appendix 1, themes 8 and 10). The "Columbia" and *Country Band March* borrowings are largely confined to particular passages in "Hawthorne." The first phrase of *Martyn* forms the heart of the principal hymn in "Hawthorne," portions of "The Alcotts," and the concluding cadence in the first half of the "human faith melody" (segment w^1); its second phrase launches the final portion of Ives's central "melody."

In handwritten emendations entered after the 1973 reprint of his *Catalogue*, Kirkpatrick added the fiddle tune "Pig Town Fling" and Ives's song *He Is There!* to the "what else?" query in "Hawthorne."[15] He also assigned the judgment "possibly" to A. F. Winnemore's minstrel tune "Stop That Knocking at My Door" (Appendix 1, theme 17) in "The Alcotts" (Ex. 5.1 c).[16] The extensive self-reference to *He Is There!* is certifiable and the fleeting allusion to "Stop That Knocking" (nearly identical rhythm and melodic contour for most of two measures) appears to be a plausible, if less certain source. Resemblances to "Pig Town Fling," however, are remote and tangential and more convincingly explained by their connections to the more fundamental motive u and its transformations in "Hawthorne."[17] In addition to noting the self-borrowing of *Country Band March* and *He Is There!* Kirkpatrick was also the first, again in the *Catalogue*, to mention a connection between the *Emerson*

Overture and *Study No. 2* and *Study No. 9* (*The Anti-Abolitionist Riots*).[18] Later, in his copious addition to Ives's *Memos*, Kirkpatrick observed a remote foreshadowing of the song *Aeschylus and Sophocles* in "Thoreau" (*Memos*, pp. 73, n. 3 and 82, n. 12).

Later discoveries of Ives borrowings

Despite indefatigable tune sleuthing, Kirkpatrick has not had the last word in lists of borrowings. Among later writers Fred Fisher offers a sizable list of possible borrowings that were not recognized by Kirkpatrick in any sense of the word. As with Kirkpatrick's attribution of "Pig Town Fling," most of Fisher's borrowings can be more feasibly attributed to other sources or as allusions or puns based on the central acknowledged or unmistakable borrowed sources. Some of Fisher's more speculative borrowings do of course share common features with the *Concord Sonata*, for example, the familial resemblance between a phrase of Samuel Webbe, Sr.'s *Consolator* ("Come, Ye Disconsolate") and the "corn field" motive (Appendix 1, theme 18), but these likenesses do not demonstrably constitute musical borrowings. Similarly, while an ascending whole-tone scale figures prominently at the opening of the sonata and in many other passages, it does not warrant identification with the opening of Bach's *Es ist genug* chorale from Cantata No. 60. On the other hand the B-A-C-H "quote" in "Hawthorne," the German spelling of B-flat, A, C, B-natural near the conclusion of the famous "strip of board" passage (p. 25, sys. 4), may be intentional.[19]

As a general rule, when a hypothetical borrowing fails to stand up on its own musical terms or to exhibit a demonstrable programmatic purpose, it will be cast out of Ives's garden of borrowings in the present volume. For these reasons most of Fisher's attributions fall in the "questionable" category. For example, the arpeggiated accompaniment to the central "verse" section (pages 8–11) in "Emerson" resembles the left hand of Chopin's "Revolutionary" Etude, op. 10, no. 12 only superficially and generically. Also, Brahms's F-sharp minor piano sonata, op. 2, which shares the opening four notes of the "human faith melody," fails Gimbel's third criterion. Its obscurity for Ives and his contemporaries excludes this fragment as a serious contender for inclusion among consciously borrowed sources.

Ex. 5.2 *Crusader's Hymn* borrowings

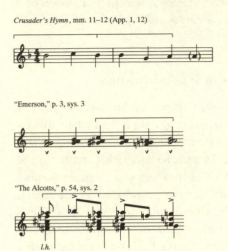

In contrast to these intriguing but ultimately discarded possibilities, two Fisher borrowings have been welcomed in this study, *Crusader's Hymn* ("Fairest Lord Jesus") (theme 12 and Ex. 5.2) and the first phrase of Beethoven's "Hammerklavier" Sonata (first movement) (theme 10 and Ex. 4.1 f). A theme based on or paraphrased from *Crusader's Hymn* (probably the "Tolerance" theme mentioned by Kirkpatrick in *Memos*, p. 199, n. 3) appears briefly early in "Emerson" (p. 2, sys. 4–5 and p. 3, sys. 3–4) before its fleeting return in "The Alcotts" (p. 54, sys. 2). The "Hammerklavier" phrase receives a place of honor in the "human faith melody" itself, immediately after Beethoven's Fifth Symphony. The "Hammerklavier" phrase featured prominently with full C major chordal statements in "The Alcotts" (p. 57, sys. 5), also strongly resembles Beethoven's piano texture; other appearances adopt Beethoven's key of B-flat major, "The Alcotts" (p. 55, sys. 2–3) and "Thoreau" (p. 68, sys. 1). The programmatic meaning is also convincing. Like the ubiquitous references to Beethoven's symphony, the "Hammerklavier" reference embodies a strong symbol of Beethoven's legitimacy and authority among Concord Transcendentalists.

Other Ives scholars have raised additional possibilities of Ives's musical borrowings in the *Concord Sonata*. Although Lowell Mason's

Bethany, a frequent and conspicuous guest in Ives's compositions, including the Second String Quartet and the Fourth Symphony, does not receive separate inclusion here, Robert Douglas Fruehwald's discovery of the musical pun which connects *Bethany* with the Foster "corn field" motive and the lyrical transformation of motive *u* in a "Thoreau" motive (Ex. 4.2 f) should not go unnoticed.[20] Thomas M. Brodhead, in addition to effectively demonstrating the frequent points of correspondence among "Hawthorne," *The Celestial Railroad*, and the second movement of the Fourth Symphony, has identified a brief but unmistakable *Celestial Railroad* borrowing in "Emerson" and less convincingly, the presence of "Peter, Peter, Pumpkin Eater" in the "Demons' Dance around the Pipe" passage in "Hawthorne" (page 23).[21]

David Michael Hertz suggests some tantalizing possible borrowings of Debussy's preludes, most convincingly the similarities in style and effect between the final page of *La Cathédrale engloutie* and a portion of the central "verse" section in "Emerson" (p. 10, sys. 1–2).[22] Ives's considerable knowledge of and indebtedness to Debussy has only recently been discovered.[23] This handbook will add another previously unrecognized but likely Debussy borrowing, the reference in "Hawthorne" (p. 38) to "Golliwogg's Cake-Walk" from *Children's Corner* (1908), a copy of which Ives owned (Appendix 1, theme 13 and Ex. 5.3). Although Ives further distorts Debussy's already syncopated ragged rhythm, he preserves the accompaniment style, the bitonal flavor, and even the precise pitches of his predecessor.

Moments later in the same extended ragtime passage in "Hawthorne" Ives offers, much less decisively, the opening incipit and other fragments of Joseph E. Howards's "Hello! Ma Baby" and the closing first-phrase ending of Harry von Tilzer's "Alexander."

Other hypothetical borrowings

This survey of real and imagined borrowings in the *Concord Sonata* will conclude with three classical sources that have not been proposed in earlier studies. Like many of the other speculative borrowings, each of these hypothetical sources poses ambiguities that make an unequivocal attribution problematic.

The first tantalizing possibility is the prospect that Ives borrowed the

Ex. 5.3 "Golliwogg's Cake-Walk" borrowing

Debussy, "Golliwogg's Cake-Walk" from *Children's Corner*, mm. 28–29 (App. 1, 13)

"Hawthorne," p. 38, sys. 1

idea to combine two triads a tritone apart from Stravinsky's famous *Petrushka* chord (Ex. 5.4). It occurs in "Emerson" (p. 7, sys. 1). While the "idea" of successive chords a tritone apart can be traced as far back as Musorgsky's Coronation Scene in *Boris Godunov* (1868–69), Rimsky-Korsakov's *Scheherazade* (1888), and more recently in Ravel's *Jeux d'eau* (1901) and Debussy's *Brouillards* (1913), Stravinsky's simultaneous presentation of bare triads separated by a tritone could be new.[24]

The strongest circumstantial evidence that might make such an influence theoretically possible is the recent discovery that the paper-type on which Ives's bitonal passage appears most likely can be dated after 1914 (see chapter 3). Completed in 1911, *Petrushka* made its American debut as a ballet in New York City early in 1916. Although the passage in question probably postdates the *Emerson Overture* and Ives's recollection that he finished the sonata by 1915, no evidence has surfaced that would firmly establish this resemblance as a conscious borrowing. The idea of two triads a tritone apart (usually A and E-flat/D-sharp) will reappear, albeit successively rather than simultaneously, later on the same page of "Emerson" (p. 7, sys. 3–4) and at the beginning and end of "Thoreau" (pp. 59 and 68).[25]

The second new classical borrowing suggested here, the opening of

Ex. 5.4 *Petrushka* borrowing

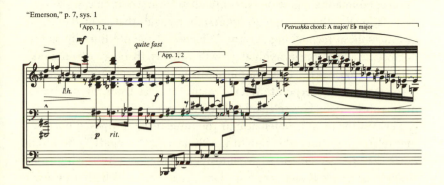

Wagner's *Prelude* to *Tristan und Isolde* (theme 11 and Ex. 4.7 a) seems a strong candidate for an intentionally borrowed theme. In contrast to the *Petrushka* fragment, the opening of Wagner's *Prelude* emerges as one of the central themes in "Emerson" and the source of considerable development in the course of the movement (see Ex. 4.7 b–f), including the thirteen-note "fugue subject" (p. 13, sys. 4 [Ex. 4.7 f] and p. 17, sys. 2) and the two eleven-note answers (p. 13, sys. 5 – p. 14, sys. 1) discussed in chapter 4. The usual *Tristan* reference encompasses six-notes; less often the borrowing consists of only the first four notes.

The central ambiguity of this borrowing is Ives's unwillingness to display the "correct" first note of Wagner's theme. In fact, in the majority of its appearances the original form and all of the inversions of the motive begin with a diminished fifth rather than Wagner's minor sixth. At other places Ives chooses more remote starting intervals. On the rare occasions when he does adopt Wagner's interval, Ives obfuscates the gesture, either by inserting a new note between the ascending sixth (Ex. 4.7 e) or by displacing the octave and thereby the audibility of the first note.

Ives complicates the Wagner reference when he almost invariably adds an additional contrapuntal line, usually the first four notes of the main "Emerson" lyric theme (Appendix 1, theme 2, shown in Ex. 4.1 b and Ex. 5.4, sys. 2–3). The strong profile of Wagner's six notes (and less often the first four), the closeness of the starting interval, and the identity of the other pitches combine to create a case for its inclusion as a conscious, albeit somewhat "hidden" borrowing. All that is missing from Gimbel's criteria is an "extramusical context," or at least a context compatible with the programmatic suggestion Ives entered in his first edition copy, R³ (old designation R²): the attempt "to suggest the struggle that seemed to go on in Emerson, in reconciling . . . the influence of the old Puritan canon, dogma, etc., with this individual growth – that is, theology vs. religion" (*Memos*, p. 199, n. 3).[26] The canonic nature of the passage is made clear by the extensive counterpoint. What remains unclear from the programmatic rubric is why Ives selected Wagner and not Bach.

Perhaps the most problematic of the three newly proposed borrowings relates to the identification of the "human faith melody"'s first four notes (Ex. 4.1 a, segment *t*), previously dismissed as a borrowing from Brahms's obscure F-sharp minor piano sonata, op. 2. Whether by accident or design these are the same four notes, on the same four pitches, as the famous French horn opening of Schubert's Ninth Symphony (Ex. 5.5).[27] Ives's predilection to base his principal and much of his secondary musical material on a pre-existent source is sufficient cause to be alerted to the possibility of a borrowing of this ubiquitous opening phrase. Additionally, it might be noted that, despite a retrospective plausibility bordering on obviousness, the recognition of Beethoven's "Hammerklavier" Sonata as a borrowed source was a belated discovery. In fact, after the opening four notes, all six of the remaining motives that form the "human faith melody" can be accounted for as derivations or prototypes of other *Concord Sonata* themes.

Despite the relative absence of documented hero worship, at least compared with Beethoven, Schubert ranked among Ives's favored composers. Of equal significance, Schubert was associated with Ives's father, George. In his "memos" Ives recalled that "Father could play, on his horn, a Franz Schubert or Steve Foster song better than many singers

Ex. 5.5 Schubert's Ninth Symphony borrowing

Schubert, Symphony No. 9 in C major, mm. 1–3

"Emerson," p. 1, sys. 1

could sing it" (*Memos*, p. 127).[28] Several of Ives's own songs are at least
partially based on Schubert's.[29] During his years at Yale he arranged
Schubert's *March Militaire* and had the opportunity to hear the New
Haven Symphony perform the orchestral music to *Rosamunde*, the
"Unfinished" Symphony (twice), and, midway through Ives's sopho-
more year, Schubert's Ninth.[30] And if he had read Daniel Gregory
Mason's panegyric on this symphony that concludes his essay on Schu-
bert in *The Romantic Composers* (1906), Ives, too, might have associated
Schubert with the acknowledged musical hero and spiritual father of the
Concord Sonata, Beethoven. It also may be relevant that the premature
death of George, Ives's hero and real life father, like Schubert's, deprived
the world of a "profounder expression":

> It is not a mere coincidence that the theme at the beginning of the develop-
> ment section so strongly suggests Beethoven's "Hymn of Joy"; the spirit is
> Beethoven's, and the spaciousness of the scheme of construction, if not
> the detail with which it is filled in, are worthy of the greatest symphonist
> . . . Death never came to an artist more untimely.[31]

The possible programmatic or symbolic significance of this opening
"human faith"-Schubert motive remains a matter of conjecture. While it
can be safely assumed that Ives knew Schubert's symphony and that he
admired Schubert's songs and associated them, along with Foster's, with
his father, the evidence remains insufficient. Four notes, frequently or
prominently placed or identically pitched, may be enough to make a firm
attribution, but not without some additional documentary or reliable
circumstantial evidence.[32]

In contrast to some fragments that grow into more recognizable phrases of borrowed melody (e.g., the "Columbia" passage in "Hawthorne" on pages 42–44), one looks in vain for another note or two of Schubert's theme or a literary clue in the form of a "memo" that would provide a more positive identification. Further, the four-note motive that opens the "human faith motive" shares the rhythm of Beethoven's Fifth Symphony motive, and its pitches (1–2–3–6 in major) are the same as the "Emerson" motive (theme 4) of the first movement (3–2–2–6–1).[33]

Thus, in the absence of further evidence, the question of whether Ives intentionally borrowed Schubert's famous opening must remain unanswered. One might also consider the caveats of Charles Rosen and view with skepticism the idea that something so potentially significant could go unnoticed after undergoing such scrutiny.

> The trouble with any criticism which discovers something in a well-known work that no one seems to have noticed before: it is not likely to be important, or to have anything to do with why the work is considered a masterpiece.[34]

The programmatic significance of the *Concord Sonata*'s musical borrowings will be explored further in chapter 6. Here it might be reiterated that Beethoven and his Fifth Symphony were revered by the Concord Transcendentalists as well as by Ives and that both Beethoven and Foster played crucial roles in Ives's early and subsequent development. Ives selected *Martyn* and *Missionary Chant* and perhaps "Columbia, the Gem of the Ocean" for their musical properties which link them to Beethoven's Fifth Symphony. Other choices, such as Ives's *Country Band March* as an appropriate circus band "secular noise," Debussy's "Golliwogg's Cake-Walk" and the "ragtime" fragments that evoke "Hello! Ma Baby" and "Alexander," and the three borrowings in the Scottish air section of "The Alcotts" ("Loch Lomond," Wagner's *Wedding March*, and "Stop That Knocking at My Door") similarly serve the program as described in Ives's various writings.

The remaining borrowings, especially the classical references, however, appear to have been chosen more for their musical properties than for their programmatic possibilities; music, as Ives stated in his own dedicatory preface, "for those who can't stand" the essays. But the absence of specific programmatic meanings should not obscure the larger meaning behind their inclusion. The act of writing a sonata, a potent symbol of the classical tradition, especially a sonata of this magnitude and scope, can easily be construed as an attempt by Ives to compete with the European masters (especially Beethoven) on their own turf. Although Ives did not acknowledge most of his classical borrowings, from Bach to Wagner to Debussy, it is their presence rather than their recognition that is required. In any event, the imagination with which Ives uses his borrowed (and original) material is ultimately far more important than their real or imagined origins.

Musical borrowings in the *Concord Sonata*
For "Abbreviations and sources of attribution" see p. 64 at end of list.

All movements

Ludwig van Beethoven: Symphony No. 5 in C Minor, op. 67 (1807–08) [H173] (I, mm. 1–4) [App. 1, theme 7] / *CS*, p. 6, sys. 2, m. 2 (RH/LH) (Ex. 4.1 a and c; Ex. 4.3; Ex. 4.4; Ex. 4.5 a–e; Ex. 4.8) [Ives 1920]
  Piano Sonata No. 29 in B-Flat Major, op. 106 ("Hammerklavier") (1817–18) [H173] (I, mm. 1–2) [App. 1, theme 9] / *CS*, p. 57, sys. 5 (RH/LH) (Ex. 4.1 a and f; Ex. 4.3 b; Ex. 4.4; Ex. 4.8) [Fisher 1981]
Simeon B. Marsh: *Martyn* ("Jesus, lover of my soul") (1834) [H35] (mm. 1–5) [App. 1, theme 8] / *CS*, p. 34, sys. 2–4 (RH/LH) (Ex. 4.1 a and d; Ex. 4.3; Ex. 4.4; Ex. 4.8) [Kirkpatrick 1960]

Questionable borrowings

Johannes Brahms: Piano Sonata No. 2 in F-Sharp Minor, op. 2 (1852) (I, m. 1) / *CS*, p. 1, sys. 1 (RH) [Fisher 1981]
Franz Schubert: Symphony No. 9 in C Major (D. 944) ("Great") (1825–26) (I, mm. 1–3) / *CS*, p. 1, sys. 1 (RH) (Ex. 5.5) [Block 1996]

"Emerson"[35]

David T. Shaw: "Columbia, the Gem of the Ocean" (1843) (see also "Hawthorne" and "The Alcotts") [H75] (mm. 1–2) [App. 1, theme 10] / *CS*, p. 2, sys. 2–3 (LH) (Ex. 4.1 g; Ex. 4.2 e) [Kirkpatrick 1960]
Richard Wagner: *Prelude* to *Tristan und Isolde* (1856–59; premiere 1865) [H189]

(mm. 1–3) [App. 1, theme 11] / *CS*, p. 1, sys. 2–3 (RH) (Ex. 4.7 a–f; Ex. 4.8) [Block 1996]

Crusader's Hymn ("Fairest Lord Jesus") (*Schlesische Volkslieder*, 1842; arr. by Richard Storrs Willis, 1850) (mm. 11–12) [App. 1, theme 12] / *CS*, p. 3, sys. 3 and p. 54, sys. 2 (RH) (Ex. 5.2) [Fisher 1981]

Ives: *Study No. 9 (The Anti-Abolitionist Riots)* (1907–13) (sys. 13–14) / *CS*, p. 1, sys. 2 (RH/LH) [Kirkpatrick 1960]

The Celestial Railroad (*c.* 1926) (m. 35) / *CS*, p. 13, sys. 1, m. 3–sys. 2, m. 1 (RH/LH) [Brodhead 1994]

Questionable borrowings

Johann Sebastian Bach: *Es ist genug* from Cantata No. 60 ("O Ewigkeit, du Donnerwort") (1723) (mm. 1–2) / *CS*, p. 1, sys. 1 (RH) [Fisher 1981]

Igor Stravinsky: *Petrushka* (1911) (rehearsal no. 49) / *CS*, p. 7, sys. 1 (RH/LH) (Ex. 5.4) [Block 1996]

Frédéric Chopin: Etude in C Minor, op. 10, no. 12 ("Revolutionary") (1830) (mm. 10–14) / *CS*, p. 10, sys. 1–2 (RH/LH) [Fisher 1994]

Claude Debussy: *La Cathédrale engloutie*, from *Douze Préludes*, Book 1 (1910) (mm. 72–83) / *CS*, p. 10, sys. 1–2 (RH/LH) [Hertz 1993]

"Hawthorne"[36]

Ives: *Scherzo: Over the Pavements* (1906–13) (mm. 125–26) and *"1, 2, 3"* (mm. 28–29) (1921) / *CS*, p. 28, sys. 3–4 (RH/LH) [Burkholder 1995]

Country Band March (1903) (mm. 5–15) / *CS*, p. 35, sys. 1, m. 1–sys. 4 (RH/LH) [Kirkpatrick 1960]

Debussy: "Golliwogg's Cake-Walk" from *Children's Corner* (1906–08) (mm. 28–29) [App. 1, theme 11] / *CS*, p. 38, sys. 1 (RH/LH) (Ex. 5.3) [Block 1996]

Shaw: "Columbia, the Gem of the Ocean" (see also "Emerson" and "The Alcotts") (mm. 1–2) [App. 1, theme 10] / *CS*, p. 43, sys. 3 – p. 44, sys. 5 (RH) (Ex. 4.1 g; Ex. 4.2 e) [Kirkpatrick 1960]

Ives: *He Is There!* (1917) (mm. 27–33) / *CS*, p. 46, sys. 2–4 (RH) [Kirkpatrick 1973]

Questionable borrowings

Traditional Fiddle Tune: "Peter, Peter, Pumpkin Eater" [H201] (mm. 1–3) / *CS*, p. 23, sys. 2–3 (RH) [Brodhead 1994]

Traditional Fiddle Tune: "Pig Town Fling" ("Warm Stuff," "Cripple Creek")
[H167] (mm. 1–3) / *CS*, p. 48, sys. 3–4 (corresponding to Kirkpatrick's
mm. 350–53) [Kirkpatrick 1973]

B-A-C-H / *CS*, p. 25, sys. 4 (LH) [Fisher 1981]

Joseph E. Howard: "Hello! Ma Baby" (1899) [H107] (m. 1) / *CS*, p. 38, sys. 4
(RH) [Block 1996]

Harry von Tilzer: "Alexander" (1904) [H94] (m. 3) / *CS*, p. 39, sys. 5 (RH)
[Block 1996]

"The Alcotts"

Charles Zeuner: *Missionary Chant* ("Ye Christian heralds, go, proclaim") [H37]
(mm. 1–3) [App. 1, theme 14] / *CS*, p. 53, sys. 1 (RH) (Ex. 4.1 e) [*Musical
Courier* 1921]

Shaw: "Columbia, the Gem of the Ocean" (see also "Emerson" and
"Hawthorne") (mm. 1–2) [App. 1, theme 10] / *CS*, p. 53, sys. 4, m. 1 (RH)
(Ex. 4.1 g; Ex. 4.2 e) [Kirkpatrick 1960]

Traditional Scottish: "Loch Lomond" ("earliest proven printing," 1881)[37]
(chorus, mm. 4–6) [App. 1, theme 15] / *CS*, p. 55, sys. 4, m. 2 (RH) (Ex.
5.1 a) [Cowell 1955]

Wagner: *Wedding March* from *Lohengrin* (1845–48; premiere 1850) (mm. 1–2)
[App. 1, theme 16 / *CS*, p. 55, sys. 4, m. 3 (RH/LH) (Ex. 5.1 b) [Cowell 1955]

Anthony F. Winnemore: "Stop That Knocking at My Door" (1843) [H136]
(mm. 1–2) [App. 1, theme 17] / *CS*, p. 56, sys. 1, mm. 1–2 (RH) (Ex. 5.1 c)
[Kirkpatrick 1973]

"Thoreau"

Stephen Foster: "Massa's in De Cold Ground" ("Down in the Corn Field")
(1852) [H121] (chorus, mm. 1–4) [App. 1, theme 18] / *CS*, p. 62, sys. 1–2
(RH) (Ex. 4.2 a) [Ives 1947]

Questionable borrowings

Debussy: *Bruyères*, from *Douze Préludes*, Book 2 (1913) (mm. 23–24) / *CS*, p. 60,
sys. 4 (RH/LH) [Hertz 1993]

Debussy: *Des Pas sur la neige*, from *Douze Préludes*, Book 1 (1910) (mm. 5–6) /
CS, p. 61, sys. 5 (RH/LH) [Hertz 1993]

Lowell Mason: *Bethany* ("Nearer, my God, to Thee") (1859) [H7] (mm. 1–2) /
CS, p. 62, sys. 1 (RH) [Fruehwald 1985]

Samuel Webbe, Sr., *Consolator* ("Come, Ye Disconsolate") (1792) (mm. 1–2) / *CS*, p. 62, sys. 1 (RH) [Fisher 1981]

Abbreviations and sources of attribution

CS   *Concord Sonata*
H   Henderson, *The Charles Ives Tunebook*
LH   left hand
RH   right hand

Block 1996. *Ives: Concord Sonata* (this handbook)
Brodhead 1994. "Ives's *Celestial Railroad* and His Fourth Symphony"
Burkholder 1995. Personal communication to author.
Cowell 1955. *Charles Ives and His Music.*
Fisher 1981. *Ives' Concord Sonata.*
Fruehwald 1985. "Motivic Transformation in the 'Thoreau' Movement of Charles Ives' *Concord Sonata*".
Hertz 1993. *Angels of Reality.*
Ives 1920. *Essays Before a Sonata*
Ives 1947. *Concord Sonata* (2nd edn)
Kirkpatrick 1960. *A Temporary Mimeographed Catalogue*
Kirkpatrick 1973. *A Temporary Mimeographed Catalogue* (handwritten emendations)
Musical Courier 1921. "Concord Unconquered." *Musical Courier* 82, no. 17 (April 28, 1921): 22

6

The program

Ives and programmaticism

In his "Prologue" to the *Essays Before a Sonata* Ives offers an inconclusive personal debate on the nature of program music. At the outset he even questions the whole enterprise:

> How far is anyone justified, be he an authority or a layman, in expressing or trying to express in terms of music (in sounds, if you like) the value of anything, material, moral, intellectual, or spiritual, which is usually expressed in terms other than music? (*Essays*, p. 3)

Ives continues this opening gambit by asking twelve additional mostly unanswered questions in which he confronts difficult philosophical issues that nearly all composers of program music and their audiences invariably face. His question (p. 4), "Does the success of program music depend more upon the program than upon the music?" still needs to be asked. One might respond that symphonies and sonatas with suggestive titles or programmatic content have indeed received more than their fair share of recognition; one might also ask whether the subject of this handbook would have received the same attention and acclaim had Ives not chosen to write his elaborate prefatory *Essays Before a Sonata* that provide a programmatic handle upon which otherwise uncomprehending listeners can begin to grasp the complex mysteries of his sonata.

By the second paragraph Ives changes the premises of his questions. Now he inquires, "Is not all music program music" and "Is not pure music, so called, representative in its essence?" The rhetorical nature of this last question may have been influenced by the comments of Daniel Gregory Mason in his then recent *Contemporary Composers* (1918), which Ives read in Asheville, North Carolina, when he drafted his essays the following year, and a book from which Ives almost certainly borrowed other ideas. In his essay on Richard Strauss, for example, Mason expresses a decided bias in favor of non-programmatic music and argues that "in all symphonic poems it is the symphonic rather than the poetic element that is chiefly responsible for the effect produced."[1]

Even when praising *Tod und Verklärung* Mason condemns Strauss's "repulsively realistic details." In later works Strauss's "love of crass realism thus early revealed has grown apace, by even steps, unfortunately, with the extraordinary powers upon which it is parasitic."[2] Perhaps some of Mason's negativism regarding Strauss and programmaticism may have rubbed off on Ives and contributed to his withdrawal from some of his original programmatic intentions and his distancing from Strauss's baser instincts.[3] In his earlier incomplete "memo" of 1913 Ives had in fact launched a rigorous programmatic description of "Hawthorne" that he would largely abandon in the "Hawthorne" essay (*Memos*, pp. 187–88). By 1920, for Ives as well as for Mason, Strauss was a composer who aimed too low: "The shot may often hit the mark, but as often rebound, and harden, if not destroy, the shooter's heart – even his soul" (*Essays*, p. 83).

For whatever reason, Ives did not in most cases offer a program that features a one-to-one correspondence between his sonata and a continuous narrative. Ives may aspire to achieve "moral goodness, intellectual power, high vitality, and strength," but he acknowledges the difficulty of attaining such lofty goals and the improbability of having his goals, even if realized, be universally understood. Although "the fear of failure need keep no one from the attempt," Ives ends the "Prologue" (p. 8) with a retreat from programmaticism: "But we would rather believe that music is beyond any analogy to word language."

Ives's approach to programmaticism shares much in common with Berlioz's pioneering and in some ways *sui generis* program symphony, the *Symphonie fantastique* (1830). Like Berlioz, Ives wrote his own program notes and distributed significant extended portions when he presented his work publicly. Although Ives had originally planned to publish his *Essays* and his sonata in one package, he eventually opted to insert liberal excerpts in the printed first edition. At the outset of this edition he inserted excerpts from the beginning and end of the "Prologue," and, following the musical text, he included representative portions of his "Epilogue," including his famous distinctions between "substance" and "manner." Directly preceding each movement Ives presented virtually all the programmatic references found in the *Essays* to the virtual exclusion of his other thoughts on the men (or, in the case of "The Alcotts," the family) that inspired his four movements.

Like Berlioz, Ives would change his thoughts on the specifics of his program over a period of several decades. In contrast to Berlioz, accretions rather than alterations to the program were the rule for Ives. Also, like most of the adopted musical revisions that Ives entered in his personal first edition copies, the adopted programmatic details appeared in the second edition (albeit in the endnotes rather than the main musical text). Although Ives began to draft revisions for a second edition of the *Essays* to complement the second edition of the music, he soon abandoned this attempt.[4]

Neither the *Symphonie fantastique* nor the *Concord Sonata* exhibits a continuous narrative program. Instead, both works offer mainly symbolic representation with some specific programmatic elements scattered intermittently throughout. The two primary functions served by Berlioz's program as summarized by Nicholas Temperley may also be applied to some degree to Ives. As an example of the first function, "to particularize meanings that were already perceptible in the music," Temperley cites the recurring *idée fixe*, which, while satisfying on its own musical terms, would not be understood to represent a woman without Berlioz's program.[5] Similarly, listeners to the *Concord Sonata* might hear how musical fragments throughout "Emerson" and "Hawthorne" evolve into a continuous extended melody in "The Alcotts" and "Thoreau," and most listeners would detect that the opening of Beethoven's frequently pronounced Fifth Symphony motive (Appendix 1, theme 7) figures prominently in Ives's sonata. Without the composer's written identification and commentary on the "human faith melody" (theme 1), however, the symbolic meaning of his Beethoven borrowing would not be readily perceived. At best its meaning might change from one generation to the next.

The second programmatic function in Berlioz's symphony noted by Temperley is that "the Program completes the story by supplying details that are not to be found in the music at all."[6] While few music lovers would deny that music can generate a profound emotional impact, an emotion like jealousy, such as that successfully embodied in Verdi's

Otello or the nameless hero of the *Symphonie fantastique*, is too specific for unequivocal musical representation without the aid of a sung text or program. For this reason Berlioz felt that the distribution of his program was "indispensable for a complete understanding of the dramatic outline of the work."[7]

Berlioz, who "well knows that music cannot replace the word, nor the pictorial art," is more concerned with describing emotions and feelings than with the attempt to convey a literal and specific programmatic narrative.[8] Ives, who similarly "would rather believe that music is beyond any analogy to word language" (*Essays*, p. 8) is also more concerned with symbolic meanings than with the representation of objects and a musical narrative. As a prefatory statement included with the *Essays* and the first edition (and reprinted as a postlude to the second edition) Ives introduces his broader programmatic goals:

> The whole is an attempt to present (one person's) impression of the spirit of transcendentalism that is associated in the minds of many with Concord, Mass., of over a half century ago. This is undertaken in impressionistic pictures of Emerson and Thoreau, a sketch of the Alcotts, and a *scherzo* supposed to reflect a lighter quality which is often found in the fantastic side of Hawthorne. The first and last movements do not aim to give any programs of the life or of any particular work of either Emerson or Thoreau, but, rather, composite pictures or impressions. (*Essays*, p. xxv)

Ives reveals his symbolic and programmatic intentions for the *Concord Sonata* in five places over a period of more than thirty years (1913–47). The first source of Ives's "extra-musical" ideas is the important 1913 "memo" discussed in chapter 3, the memo in which Ives recalled playing the entire sonata the previous year for Max Smith (*Memos*, pp. 187–88). In its incomplete final paragraph Ives offers the beginning of what may have been a full narrative description of the musical events in "Hawthorne." The second source is the *Essays*, the programmatic excerpts of which are included in the first and second editions of the sonata prior to each movement. The third source of programmatic information can be found in the notes that Ives entered in some of his first edition copies (1921–40).[9] The fourth source is Ives's descriptions in the "memos" of the 1930s to which might be added his response to John Kirkpatrick's questionnaire in 1935 and the thoughts he shared with the pianist in their meetings (1937–39) (*Memos*, pp. 81–83 and 188–204).

Finally, Ives included a number of programmatic references in the performance notes for the second edition published in 1947 as well as a number of programmatic suggestions that remained unpublished.[10]

"Emerson"

Ives's central "impression" of Ralph Waldo Emerson (1803–82) might be phrased something like this: here is a man of substance who deserves a movement that somehow manages to convey it. Although Ives offers few specific parallels between his music and the life and work of Emerson, he does provide enough information to suggest that the "Emerson" movement constitutes an attempt to musically realize the composer's idealized picture of the Concord sage and to achieve a parallel between Emerson's frequently difficult literary style and Ives's comparably difficult musical modernism. To put a programmatic face on "Emerson," it is perhaps not too far-fetched to interpret Ives's movement as a series of variations on lecture themes (albeit untitled), interspersed and intertwined with passages of Emerson's verse.[11]

It has not gone unnoticed that Ives, when describing Emerson, is also to a large extent describing his own work and ideals.[12] Clearly, Emerson is the kind of man Ives aspired to be, a man of substance over manner in search of truth:

> Emerson is more interested in what he perceives than in his expression of it. He is a creator whose intensity is consumed more with the substance of his creation than with the manner by which he shows it to others. . . It must be remembered that truth was what Emerson was after – not strength of outline or even beauty, except insofar as they might reveal themselves naturally in his explorations towards the infinite. (*Essays*, p. 21)

Support for the notion that the "Emerson" movement might be viewed as a set of free-wheeling variations on several lecture topics with poetic interludes can be found more directly in Ives's description of Emerson's essays. The unpublished performance note at one time contemplated for the second edition (for p. 6, sys. 1) offers an example in which Ives describes how to realize a programmatic gesture. It also provides some tangible evidence that Ives is making an analogy between Emerson's oratorical lecture style and his own musical rhetoric.

... the eighth note [the A before the *] may be played as fast as possible but as the last D# in RH and G# in LH is struck, the right hand may be lifted up, round & down on to highest A which will cause a slight pause in the speed – and as "the village preacher (perhaps Emerson) will bring his hand down on the pulpit as the big point of the "Text" is given out. This is our Text." (Ives Collection, f342)

Appropriately, the "big point" that follows is none other than an especially turbulent statement of Beethoven's Fifth Symphony and "Hammerklavier" openings in their "human faith" context.[13]

Ives's defense of Emerson's writings (more like lectures than polished prose) might also be used to challenge the charges of disunity and incoherence directed towards Ives's music, especially those directed against difficult pieces such as "Emerson."

> His [Emerson's] underlying plan of work seems based on the large unity of a series of particular aspects of a subject rather than on the continuity of its expression. As thoughts surge to his mind, he fills the heavens with them, crowds them in, if necessary, but seldom arranges them along the ground first. Among class-room excuses for Emerson's imperfect coherence and lack of unity is one that remembers that his essays were made from lecture notes. His habit, often, in lecturing was to compile his ideas as they came to him on a general subject in scattered notes, and, when on the platform, to trust to the mood of the occasion to assemble them. (*Essays*, p. 22)

After defending the accusation of vagueness, frequently voiced at Emerson, as "an indication of nearness to a perfect truth" (*Essays*, p. 22), Ives concludes that "so close a relation exists between his content and expression, his substance and manner, that if he were more definite in the latter he would lose power in the former" (*Essays*, pp. 29–30). Stuart Feder attributes Ives's decision to write essays as a sign of his debt to his predecessor, the great essayist, and considers Ives's "scholarly, reasoned, and inspirational texture peppered with quotes and epigrams – almost a caricature of Emerson's style."[14]

In a direct attempt to create a musical analogy with Emerson's writing, in the first edition Ives labeled a number of the sections outlined in chapter 4 either "prose" or "verse." The prose sections, like written prose, tend to be less metrical and tuneful and more dissonant than their verse counterparts. The section from pages 8–11 (section 3) is the longest "verse" passage in "Emerson."[15] Two sections which begin with the most extended statements of the "Emerson" lyric theme, sections 2 and 7, are also labeled verse by Ives in the first edition.[16] In the second edition Ives retained a label only for section 4. In another parallel between the musical and the literary it might be noted that just as Emerson bases his poetry on the philosophical ideas of his prose, so does Ives create his verse material out of his musical prose.[17]

Earlier in his "Emerson" essay (*Essays*, p. 30) Ives expressed the view that Emerson's "flashes of transcendent beauty" and his revelations "approach as near the divine as Beethoven in his most inspired moments." Ives concludes the essay (*Essays*, p. 36) by again equating his literary hero, Emerson, with his musical hero, Beethoven. This leads Ives to explain why he links Beethoven's Fifth Symphony with the "common heart" of Concord:

> There is an "oracle" at the beginning of the Fifth Symphony; in those four notes lies one of Beethoven's greatest messages. We would place its translation above the relentlessness of fate knocking at the door, above the greater human message of destiny, and strive to bring it towards the spiritual message of Emerson's revelations, even to the "common heart" of Concord – the soul of humanity knocking at the door of the divine mysteries, radiant in the faith that it *will* be opened – and the human become the divine!
> (*Essays*, p. 36)

In this last sentence Ives helps the listener interpret the idea behind the music in the final minutes of "Emerson." Clearly, Ives is trying to capture a closing musical serenity analogous to the conclusion of Emerson's essays and lectures.[18] In this context Ives's reflective transformation of Beethoven, a "translation above the relentlessness of fate knocking at the door" and "towards the spiritual message of Emerson's revelations" and "the 'common heart' of Concord," can be better understood.

Nearly four decades later Kirkpatrick recalled a conversation with Harmony Ives in which he asked whether Ives "consciously modeled his life on Emerson's."[19] Mrs. Ives "didn't think he would have thought of it that way, because he would have thought that he was a little unworthy to set out to model his life on Emerson's – he had such an exalted idea of Emerson." Nevertheless, Harmony did acknowledge that her husband "was very intimately and very deeply influenced by him." Nowhere is that influence more devoutly realized than in the "Emerson" movement of the *Concord Sonata*.

"Hawthorne"

In his brief essay on "Hawthorne" (*Essays*, pp. 39–40) Ives resists the judgment that Nathaniel Hawthorne (1804–64) was "a poet of greater imaginative impulse than Emerson or Thoreau." To circumvent this inference Ives writes that Hawthorne "was not a greater poet, possibly, than they – but a greater artist." For Ives, Hawthorne surpasses the artistry of Edgar Allan Poe and Tchaikovsky, who "occasionally" cater to their audiences. Hawthorne also possesses stronger "intellectual muscles" than Ravel or Stravinsky, who convey "a kind of false beauty obtained by artistic monotony." In sharp contrast to Emerson's substance "and even his manner," which "has little to do with a designed effect," however, the "more artistic" Hawthorne is nonetheless "more considerate" of his constituency.

The composer's sentiments transparently lean more heavily towards Emerson's substance than Hawthorne's manner, however much Ives admires the latter's artistry. This becomes increasingly evident when, later in the "Hawthorne" essay, Ives again contrasts Hawthorne's artistry with Emerson's greater spiritual substance. Although Ives acknowledges that some readers will consider Hawthorne "wiser in a more practical way, and so more artistic than Emerson," he openly expresses his greater love and respect for the Concord Bard (*Essays*, pp. 41–42).

Perhaps for this reason Ives does not attempt to present a "comprehensive conception of Hawthorne, either in words or music." According to Ives, such a conception "must have for its basic theme something that has to do with the influence of sin upon the conscience." Instead of addressing this "fundamental part," however, Ives settles for something less profound. More modestly, he attempts "to suggest some of his [Hawthorne's] wilder, fantastical adventures into the half-childlike, half-fairylike phantasmal realms."

In the final paragraph of the 1913 "memo" (*Memos*, pp. 187–88) Ives begins a programmatic description that breaks off before the end of section 1, somewhere between pages 26 and 33 (most likely about page 28). At the end of his "Hawthorne" essay Ives offers a few possibilities about which of the various unspecified passages may have "something to do with" certain "Hawthorne" stories or programmatic elements.[20] Those that pertain to the hymn and march segment at the end of section 1 and the beginning of section 2 (pages 33–37) are located more exactly and described in more detail in the published performance notes.[21] In several first edition copies and unpublished performance notes Ives either clarified the programmatic description of the 1913 memo or planted new programmatic clues for other passages.[22]

In the 1933 "memo" Ives recalled that "Hawthorne"

> started principally with the *Celestial Railroad* idea – (in two pieces for piano, take-offs: *The Celestial Railroad*, around pages . . . , *The Slaves' Shuffle*, pages . . . , [also the] *Demons' Dance around the Pipe*, – and were written on our first vacation at Pell's, September 1909. (*Memos*, p. 81)[23]

Without providing evidence such as Ives's notations in first edition copies, Kirkpatrick speculates that the "Slaves' Shuffle" may be "the second ragtime (starting on p. 37 of the revised edition)" (*Memos*, p. 81, n. 7).

In the early 1920s Ives recast and reordered much of "Hawthorne" into a new piano piece generally known as *The Celestial Railroad*. Thomas M. Brodhead has shown that, contrary to the accepted chronology suggested by Ives and accepted by Kirkpatrick, *The Celestial Railroad*, which closely parallels the second movement of the Fourth Symphony, should be viewed more as a prototype than a byproduct of the symphony.[24] According to Brodhead, the symphonic movement performed in 1927, previously thought to have been worked out by 1916, actually post-dated the composition of *The Celestial Railroad* in the mid-1920s.

Using Henry Bellamann's 1927 *Pro Musica Quarterly* program notes, which in Kirkpatrick's view were "obviously based on conversations with Ives," Brodhead offers a program of *The Celestial Railroad* that can account for much of the action in Hawthorne's story of that name.[25] Although Ives acknowledged *The Celestial Railroad* as a starting point, other Hawthorne tales posed in the *Essays* also appear in the "Hawthorne" movement. As a result of Ives's move towards a more exclusive program for *The Celestial Railroad*, i.e., a movement based on a single story, some of the overlapping material between the two piano works must be reinterpreted. For example, the hymn tune in the church (*Martyn*) and the "secular noises" of the circus parade (Ives's *Country Band March*) in "Hawthorne," pages 34–35, serve in *The Celestial Railroad* to mark the pilgrim's stylish arrival by train rather than on foot, the ferry boarding in Beulah Land, and the end of the narrator's dream when he realizes that Mr. Smooth-it-Away is none other than the Devil incarnate.[26]

"The Alcotts"

In his 1935 response to Kirkpatrick's question, "Does 'Emerson' contain any examples of melody built on pre-existing words?" Ives's "No" applies to "Thoreau" as well as "Emerson."[27] After completing this disclaimer, Ives concedes that, on the other hand, "Hawthorne" and "The Alcotts" do

> try to suggest something in the tales, incidences, or more definite characteristics of the authors. For instance, the Alcott piece tries to catch something of old man Alcott's – the great talker's – sonorous thought. (*Memos*, p. 191)

When compared with "Emerson" and "Hawthorne," "The Alcotts" is indeed sonorous. And no doubt Ives considered Bronson Alcott (1799–1888), the father of Louisa May, somewhat too narrowly as "Concord's greatest talker" rather than as a man who left a distinguished literary legacy. Ives's view of the Alcott patriarch as an idealist "accustomed to wander around in the visionary unknown," contrasts markedly with his view of Bronson's famous and more earthly daughter who did "not accept the father as a prototype," a woman who inherited "but few of her father's qualities" (*Essays*, pp. 45–46).

If the dense, dissonant, and complex style of "Emerson" paralleled to some extent the life and substantive thought of its literary model, Ives's simpler and more consonant musical portrait of the "common" world of Bronson Alcott's Concord stands as a metaphor for the legacy of Ives's father, George. Like the man portrayed in Ives's essay on the senior Alcott, George Ives was an idealist who possessed "some substantial virtues, even if he couldn't make a living" (p. 46). Also in common with Bronson (according to Ives's essay) George died leaving a creative legacy with his children rather than a body of lasting artistic work. Although he did not make a living from his art, Charles Ives, unlike the admirable but non-prototypical fathers, George and Bronson, managed to provide well for his family.

In the final paragraph of his "Alcotts" essay Ives notes that he is not intending to attempt a musical portrait of "the philosophic raptures of

Bronson Alcott." Indeed, in contrast to the relatively rich picture of "Emerson," "Hawthorne," and "Thoreau" portrayed in his *Essays*, Ives's literary "sketch" and other remarks on "The Alcotts" in his *Memos* and the single published Performance Note do not add up to an extensive programmatic portrait of Bronson and his clan.[28]

Nevertheless, the singing of family hymns described in Ives's essay on "The Alcotts" is especially clear in the hymn-like paraphrase of *Missionary Chant* at the opening of the movement. In the "memo" of "1923 or later" that he entered on the flyleaves of Lawrence Gilman's first edition copy (R[4]), Ives offers a programmatic explanation of the bitonal passage early in the movement (p. 53, sys. 2 and 3).

> The left hand is in A♭ – in that key – no other key – keeps that key – is that key – it intends, does, [is] meant to do that, couldn't do anything else, and will always put the player's left-hand-mind in that nice key of A♭ and nothing else (for old man Alcott likes to talk in A♭, and Sam Staples likes to have his say over the fence in B♭). (*Memos*, p. 191)

Furthermore, in the *Essays* (p. 47) Ives takes programmatic note of "the little old spinet piano Sophia Thoreau gave to the Alcott children, on which Beth played the old Scotch airs, and played at the Fifth Symphony."[29] Still more helpfully, Ives acknowledges and names the central musical theme in his sonata, the "human faith melody," a theme that is fully realized for the first time in this movement. He also hints at the relationship he wants to convey between his "human faith melody" and Beethoven's famous "oracle":

> All around you, under the Concord sky, there still floats the influence of that human-faith-melody – transcendent and sentimental enough for the enthusiast or the cynic, respectively – reflecting an innate hope, a common interest in common things and common men – a tune the Concord bards are ever playing while they pound away at the immensities with a Beethoven-like sublimity, and with, may we say, a vehemence and perseverance, for that part of greatness is not so difficult to emulate. (*Essays*, pp. 47–48)[30]

"Thoreau"

At the conclusion of his Thoreau essay (*Essays*, pp. 67–69) Ives offers a narrative more complete and more detailed than his programmatic remarks in essays on Emerson, Hawthorne, or the Alcotts. While the explicit program as described in the *Essays* is Henry David Thoreau's (1817–62) "thought on an autumn day of Indian summer at Walden" (p. 67) Ives's broader theme in both his "Thoreau" essay and movement is Thoreau's process of becoming one with Nature. Before the entrance of the flute, Thoreau's acceptance of Nature, as embodied in many serene passages bordering on metrical indefinition and timelessness, is contrasted by several rhythmically restless and dynamically turbulent passages that reveal Thoreau's moodiness and unwillingness to submit to Nature's call.

A performance note to the second edition associated with pages 62, 65, and 68 marks the second occasion in which Ives specifies a musical borrowing (the only other named reference is Beethoven's Fifth Symphony). When Ives refers to the Elm Tree "humming a phrase from 'Down in the Corn Field,'" he no doubt refers to the chorus of Stephen Foster's "Massa's in De Cold Ground" (Appendix 1, theme 18 and Ex. 4.2 a) which was published two years before *Walden* in 1854. The connecting programmatic link is Thoreau's reference to "corn" in the following passage near the outset of "Sounds": "I grew in those seasons like corn in the night."[31] Although in the song *Thoreau* Ives refers to his subject in the third person ("He grew in those seasons like corn in the night"), he directly acknowledged Thoreau's "Sounds" (from *Walden*) as his source. The song also strengthens the connection between Foster and Thoreau, since Ives places the opening of Foster's "corn field" chorus in the piano part under the very next vocal phrase, "rapt in revery."

In the "Epilogue" to the *Essays* (p. 82) Ives contrasts Debussy's "week-end flights in country aesthetics" and "sensual sensuousness" with Thoreau's genuine oneness with Nature and "spiritual sensuousness." In view of the striking parallels between the "Thoreau" movement and Debussy's musical style (e.g., the whole-tone chords on p. 59, sys. 3), Ives's prose comparison perhaps reveals a compensatory attempt to distance himself from his musical contemporary and attain a rapport with Nature through a musical style that more closely approaches Thoreau's greater substance.[32] In his skewed comparison (p. 82) between Debussy and Thoreau Ives offers another "corn" analogy that may help clarify his decision to borrow Foster's "corn field" chorus: "We might offer the suggestion that Debussy's content would have been worthier his manner if he had hoed corn or sold news-papers for a living."

The entrance of the flute near the end of "Thoreau" is especially meaningful programmatically. Ives certainly knew that Thoreau played the flute and brought it with him to Walden.[33] Further, although he offers an optional version for piano alone, in the published performance notes for this passage Ives editorializes that "Thoreau much prefers to hear the flute over Walden."

Throughout his "Thoreau" essay Ives emphasizes the sounds of nature and Thoreau's musical qualities as "a great musician, not because he played the flute but because he did not have to go to Boston to hear 'the Symphony'" (sounds Thoreau had at his disposal at Walden simply by listening to Nature). In Ives's portrait of a "musical" writer Thoreau is "divinely conscious of the enthusiasm of Nature, the emotion of her rhythm, and the harmony of her solitude" (*Essays*, p. 51). The character-istic lyrical nature throughout "Thoreau" and its reflective triumph at its close further exemplifies the qualities of Thoreau (the man) as musi-cally realized by Ives.

Feder notes that the "tone of much of the writing [in the "Thoreau" essay] is not only that of eulogy but also that of polemic and apology" and that Ives "deals with some of Thoreau's least attractive traits." Feder also writes of a "fused image of Thoreau and George Ives," especially when, "at the close of the *Concord Sonata*, George's instrument is heard once again . . . the flute of family legend."[34] Other parallels between George and Thoreau are difficult to perceive directly in the music, but for some the "Thoreau" essay will help make Ives's sublime musical por-trait more vivid and moving.[35]

"Although he could not easily expose it," Ives's Thoreau, like Ives's Beethoven, is an inspired artist who in his "greatest moments" could "express profound truths and deep sentiment" (*Essays*, p. 51). In one respect Thoreau even surpasses Emerson's place as Ives's soul mate. Not only was Thoreau a great artist (and, in contrast to Emerson, a great musician), he was also that "reassuring and true friend" who succored Ives in his time of grief and despair, "one 'low' day, when the sun had gone down, long, long before sunset" (*Essays*, p. 67).

The unpublished notes for the final page, keyed to the pagination of the first edition (in contrast to the performance note paginations in the earlier movements), Ives remarks that the half-notes marked "echo" (at the end of sys. 2 and 4 on the final page) "are but echoes which may be sometimes omitted [as they are in the first edition] though Henry [Thoreau] quite probably would often turn with grief and sorrow when the echoes would not sing to him over the pond."[36]

Ives's sensitivity to the difficulties of conveying programmatic content and having one's "extra-musical" ideas be understood may have led to his minimizing of the *Concord Sonata* program between the work's inception around 1910 and the composition of the *Essays* ten years later. After its publication and distribution in 1921, however, Ives would reconsider programmatic aspects and include new additions in his *Memos* and Performance Notes for the second edition.

Ideologies in favor of "absolute" music may have similarly prompted Mahler to equivocate on the programmatic content of his early symphonies. Within a few years after Mahler's death (1911) and the premiere of *Rite of Spring* (1913) Stravinsky launched a crusade to remove the memory of the narrative elements and programmatic underpinning that clearly inspired the work in its original form as a ballet. Ives was not impervious to the ideological seeds that took root in the late nineteenth century, a view which held that so-called absolute music was more deserving of prestige than program music. Mason's criticisms of Strauss's tone poems quoted earlier in this chapter fall in this popular ideological tradition.

Henry Cowell also minimizes the programmatic aspects of works such as the *Concord Sonata* and the Fourth Symphony, concluding "that ultimately the music stands independent of any literary or other extra-musical connection."[37] In a similar vein some writers of Cowell's generation dismissed Berlioz's program as a "promotional aid" or "as an excuse for using up a lot of available material."[38] There can be no doubt that musical analysis which neglects Ives's programmatic motivations misses an opportunity to obtain potential truths and insights not available elsewhere. Mendelssohn considered what music expresses not to be "too indefinite to be put into words, but on the contrary, too definite"; Berlioz considered the language of instrumental music to be "richer, more varied, less restricted, and by its very indefiniteness, incomparably more powerful."[39] Recent writings have articulated that pure, autonomous, and absolute music is a fiction much in need of re-examination and challenge; a process in which Ives's programmaticism should play a significant role.[40]

APPENDIX I

Concord Sonata *themes*

Original themes

1 "human faith melody," p. 57, sys. 4–5

See Exx. 4.1 a, 4.3, 4.4, 4.6, and 4.8.

2 main "Emerson" lyric theme, p. 5, sys. 1

Slowly and quietly

See Exx. 4.1 b, 4.2 c, 4.7 c, and 4.8.

3 Henry Cowell's lyric motive
  a chromatic prototype (p. 1, sys. 1)

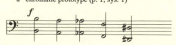

See Exx. 4.2 b and 4.8.

b diatonic / pentatonic form (p. 8, sys. 1)

See Exx. 4.2 d and 4.8.

4 "Emerson" motive (p. 1, sys. 2)

See Ex. 4.8.

5 "Thoreau 1" (p. 59, sys. 2)

6 "Thoreau 2" (p. 60, sys. 2–3)

Musical borrowings

7 Beethoven, Fifth Symphony (I, mm. 1–4)

See Exx. 4.1 c, 4.5 a, and 4.8.

8 Marsh, *Martyn* (mm. 1–5)

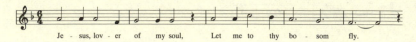

Je - sus, lov - er   of my soul,   Let me to   thy bo - som   fly.

See Exx. 4.1 d, 4.3, 4.4, and 4.8.

9 Beethoven, "Hammerklavier" Sonata (I, mm. 1–2)

See Exx. 4.1 f, 4.3, 4.4, and 4.8.

10 Shaw, "Columbia, the Gem of the Ocean," mm. 1–2

Oh Co-lum - bia, the gem of the o - cean,   (The)

See Exx. 4.1 g and 4.2 e ("Emerson," "Hawthorne," and "The Alcotts").

11 Wagner, *Prelude* to *Tristan und Isolde* (mm. 1–3)

See Exx. 4.3 and 4.4 ("Emerson").

12 *Crusader's Hymn* (mm. 11–12)
    (See no. 14, *Missionary Chant*)

Thee   will I hon_____ or, (Thee)

See Ex. 5.2 ("Emerson" and "The Alcotts").

13 Debussy, "Golliwogg's Cake-Walk" from *Children's Corner* (mm. 28–29)

See Ex. 5.3 ("Hawthorne").

14 Zeuner, *Missionary Chant* (mm. 2–3)

Ye Chris-tian her - alds,   go, pro-claim

See Ex. 4.1 e ("The Alcotts").

15 Traditional Scottish: "Loch Lomond" (chorus, mm. 4–6)

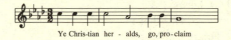

But me and my true love will nev - er meet a - gain, on the

See Ex. 5.1 a ("The Alcotts").

16 Wagner, *Wedding March* from *Lohengrin* (mm. 1–2)

Treu - lich ge - führt

See Ex. 5.1 b ("The Alcotts").

17 Winnemore, "Stop That Knocking at My Door" (mm. 1–2)

I   once did _ lub a co - lord Gal _ Whose

See Ex. 5.1 c ("The Alcotts").

18 Foster, "Down in the Corn Field," from "Massa's in De Cold Ground" (chorus, mm. 1–4)

Down   in   de corn - field   Hear that mourn-ful sound:

See Ex. 4.2 a ("Thoreau").

Self-borrowings

19 Ives: *Study No. 9* (sys. 13–14) ("Emerson")
20 Ives: *The Celestial Railroad* (m. 35) ("Hawthorne")
21 a Ives: *Scherzo: Over the Pavements* (mm. 125–26) ("Hawthorne")
     b Ives: *"1, 2, 3"* (mm. 28–29) ("Hawthorne")
22 Ives: *Country Band March* (mm. 5–15) ("Hawthorne")
23 Ives: *He Is There!* (mm. 27–33) ("Hawthorne")

Questionable borrowings

24 Brahms: Piano Sonata No. 2 in F-Sharp Minor (m. 1) (all movements)
25 Schubert: Symphony No. 9 in C Major (mm. 1–3) (Ex. 5.5) (all movements)
26 Bach: *Es ist genug* (mm. 1–2) ("Emerson")
27 Stravinsky: *Petrushka* (rehearsal no. 49) (Ex. 5.4) ("Emerson")
28 Chopin: Etude in C Minor, op. 10, no. 12 (mm. 10–14) ("Emerson")
29 Debussy: *La Cathédrale engloutie*, from *Préludes*, Book 1 (mm. 72–83) ("Emerson")
30 Traditional fiddle tune: "Peter, Peter, Pumpkin Eater" (mm. 1–3) ("Hawthorne")
31 Traditional fiddle tune: "Pig Town Fling" (m. 13) ("Hawthorne")
32 B-A-C-H ("Hawthorne")
33 Howard: "Hello! Ma Baby" (m. 1) ("Hawthorne")
34 Tilzer: "Alexander" (m. 3) ("Hawthorne")
35 Debussy: *Bruyères*, from *Préludes*, Book 2 (mm. 23–24) ("Thoreau")
36 Debussy: *Des Pas sur la neige*, from *Préludes*, Book 2 (mm. 5–6) ("Thoreau")
37 Mason: *Bethany* (mm. 1–2) ("Thoreau")
38 Webbe: *Consolator* (mm. 1–2) ("Thoreau")

See the table "Musical borrowings in the *Concord Sonata*" for more details on nos. 7–38 (above, pp. 61–64).

APPENDIX II

Formal and thematic outline

"Emerson"

Section 1: "Prose" (p. 1, sys. 1–p. 4, sys. 5)
[Appendix 1, themes 1–4, 7–12, 18–19, 26?]
Section 2: "Verse" (p. 5, sys. 1–p. 7, sys. 4)
[Appendix 1, themes 1–2, 3b–4, 7, 9, 11, 27?]
Section 3: "Verse" (p. 8, sys. 1–p. 11, sys. 4)
[Appendix 1, themes 1, 3b, 7, 28–29?]
Section 4: "Prose" (p. 12, sys. 1–p. 13, sys. 3)
[Appendix 1, themes 1–2, 3b–4, 7, 20]
Section 5: "Prose" (p. 13, sys. 4–p. 14, sys. 2, m. 1)
[Appendix 1, themes 2, 11]
Section 6: "Prose" (p. 14, sys. 2, m. 2–p. 16, sys. 2)
[Appendix 1, themes 1–2, 4, 7, 11]
Section 7: "Verse" to "Prose" (p. 16, sys. 3–p. 18,
sys. 1, m. 1) [Appendix 1, themes 1–2, 4, 11]
Section 8: "Prose" (p. 18, sys. 1, m. 2–p. 19, sys. 4)
[Appendix 1, themes 1–2, 4, 7, 9, 11]

"Hawthorne"

Section 1 (pp. 21–34)
Part 1: Introduction (p. 21, sys. 1–p. 24, sys. 4)
[Appendix 1, motive *u*, themes 1, 30–31?]
Part 2: Strip of Board (p. 25, sys. 1–p. 26, sys. 1)
[Appendix 1, theme 1, 32?]
Part 3: Ragtime I and "Human Faith" (p. 26, sys. 2–p. 34, sys. 2, m. 1)
[Appendix 1, motive *u*, themes 1, 7, 9, 21 a–b]

Section 2 (pp. 34–42)
Part 1: *Martyn* (p. 34, sys. 2, m. 2–p. 35, sys. 1, m. 3)
[Appendix 1, motive *u*, themes 1, 7–8]

Part 2: *Country Band March* (p. 35, sys. 1, m. 3–p. 37, sys. 1, m. 1)
    [Appendix 1, motive *u*, themes 7, 22]
Part 3: Ragtime II and Tone Clusters (p. 37, sys. 1, m. 2–p. 42, sys. 2)
    [Appendix 1, motive *u*, themes 1, 13, 33–34?]

Section 3 (pp. 42–51)
Part 1: Variations on "Columbia" (p. 42, sys. 3–p. 46, sys. 5, m. 1)
    [Appendix 1, themes 1, 7–8, 10, 23]
Part 2: Coda – Return to "Human Faith" (p. 46, sys. 5, m. 2–p. 51, sys. 5)
    [Appendix 1, motive *u*, themes 1, 7, 9–10]

"The Alcotts"

Section 1 (p. 53, sys. 1–p. 55, sys. 3, m. 1)
    [Appendix 1, themes 1 (*t–z*), 12, 14]
Section 2 (p. 55, sys. 3, m. 2–p. 56, sys. 4)
    [Appendix 1, themes 15–17]
Section 3 (p. 56, sys. 5–p. 57, sys. 5)
    [Appendix 1, theme 1 (*t–z*)]

"Thoreau"

Section 1 (p. 59, sys. 1–p. 60, sys. 2, m. 1)
    [Appendix 1, themes 5, 18)
Section 2 (p. 60, sys. 2, m. 2–p. 61, sys. 5)
    [Appendix 1, theme 6]
Section 3 (p. 62, sys. 1–4)
    [Appendix 1, theme 18]
Section 4 (p. 62, sys. 5–p. 64, sys. 4)
    [Appendix 1, motive *u*, themes 1, 6–8, and Ex. 4.2 f]
Section 5 (p. 64, sys. 5–p. 65, sys. 5 [fermata])
    [Appendix 1, motive *u*, themes 1, 6, 18, and Ex. 4.2 f]
Section 6 (p. 65, sys. 5 [after fermata]–p. 66, sys. 4)
    [Appendix 1, themes 1, 5–6, 18]
Section 7 (p. 67, sys. 1–p. 68, sys. 5)
    [Appendix 1, themes 1 (*t–z*), 3 b, 18]

Notes

1 Introduction

1   Henry Bellamann, "Reviews: 'Concord, Mass., 1840–1860' (A Piano Sonata by Charles E. Ives)," *Double Dealer* 2 (October 1921): 166–69.

2   J. Peter Burkholder, *Charles Ives*, ix.

3   Paul Rosenfeld, "Ives's Concord Sonata," *Modern Music* 16, no. 2 (January–February 1939): 109–12; Lawrence Gilman, "Music: A Masterpiece of American Music Heard Here for the First Time," *New York Herald Tribune*, January 21, 1939, 9. The above and other reviews of *Concord Sonata* performances in 1938 and 1939 are reprinted in their entirety (compiled by Geoffrey Block), in *Charles Ives and His World*, J. Peter Burkholder, ed., 313–37.

4   The formal title of the second edition is *Piano Sonata No. 2 ("Concord, Mass., 1840–1860")* (New York: Arrow Music Press, 1947). In an interesting turn of events, Associated Music, which acquired the sonata from Arrow Music in 1964, eventually became a subsidiary of G. Schirmer, the company that anonymously engraved the first edition in 1920.

5   Although recorded in 1945, the Kirkpatrick pressing, issued on 78 rpm, Columbia MM-749, was not released until 1948; the performance was reissued on 33 1/3 rpm, Columbia ML-4250, in 1950. See Richard Warren, *Charles E. Ives: Discography* (New Haven: Historical Sound Recordings, Yale University Library, 1972), 68.

6   Ives, *Essays Before a Sonata* (New York: The Knickerbocker Press, 1920). Ives's dedicatory preface opposite the copyright page, although widely circulated in profiles on the composer, was not reprinted in subsequent editions of the *Essays* (future page references are keyed to the 1970 edition).

7   Gilbert Chase, *America's Music: From the Pilgrims to the Present* (New York: McGraw-Hill, 1955; rev. 2nd ed., 1966; rev. 3rd ed., Urbana and Chicago: University of Illinois Press, 1987).

8   Henry Cowell and Sidney Cowell, *Charles Ives and His Music*; Stuart Feder, *Charles Ives*; Wolfgang Rathert, *The Seen and Unseen*.

9 Fred Fisher, *Ives' Concord Sonata*; Felix Meyer, *"The Art of Speaking Extravagantly."* See also the Select bibliography.

10 The most thorough survey of Ives's gradual recognition from 1921 to 1974 is Frank R. Rossiter, *Charles Ives and His America*, 191–310.

11 Elliott Carter, "The Case of Mr. Ives," *Modern Music* 16 (1939): 172–76; repr. in *The Writings of Elliott Carter: An American Composer Looks at Modern Music*, ed. Else Stone and Kurt Stone (Bloomington: Indiana University Press, 1977), 48–51; Maynard Solomon, "Charles Ives: Some Questions of Veracity," *Journal of the American Musicological Society* 40 (1987): 443–70.

12 Gayle Sherwood, "The Choral Works of Charles Ives: Chronology, Style, and Reception" (Ph.D. diss., Yale University, 1995) and Sherwood, "Questions and Veracities: Reassessing the Chronology of Ives's Choral Works." *Musical Quarterly* 78 (1994): 429–47.

13 See Geoffrey Block, "Remembrance of Dissonances Past."

14 For the former view see Carter, "The Case of Mr. Ives." For the latter view see especially J. Peter Burkholder, *All Made of Tunes*; also Dennis Marshall, "Charles Ives's Quotations: Manner or Substance?" *Perspectives of New Music* 6 (1968): 45–56, repr. in *Perspectives on American Composers*, ed. Benjamin Boretz and Edward T. Cone (New York: W. W. Norton, 1971), 13–24.

15 For a survey of Beethoven's impact on Ives see Geoffrey Block, "Ives and the 'Sounds That Beethoven Didn't Have'." The influential "anxiety of influence" theory was developed by literary critic Harold Bloom in *The Anxiety of Influence: A Theory of Poetry* (New York: Oxford University Press, 1973). The most substantial application of Bloom's to musical modernists (but excluding Ives) is Joseph N. Straus, *Remaking the Past: Musical Modernism and the Influence of the Tonal Tradition* (Cambridge, Mass.: Harvard University Press, 1990). See also David Michael Hertz, *Angels of Reality*, 15–24 and Kevin Korsyn, "Towards a New Poetics of Musical Influence," *Music Analysis* 10 (1991): 3–72.

16 Burkholder makes the point that "it is Concord, not Transcendentalism, that is the connecting thread between the four movements." Burkholder, *Charles Ives*, 30.

17 See Appendix 1, themes 8, 14, 10, 17, 16, 12, and 18, respectively. Exceptions are limited to Claude Debussy's "Golliwogg's Cake-Walk" from *Children's Corner* (1906–08) in "Hawthorne" (theme 13) and the Scottish ballad "Loch Lomond" (*c*. 1881) in "The Alcotts" (theme 15). For a complete list of borrowings, see the table on pp. 61–64.

18 For example, see Anthony Newcomb, "Once More 'Between Absolute and

Program Music': Schumann's Second Symphony," *19th Century Music* 7 (1984): 233–50.

19 Kurt Stone, "Ives's Fourth Symphony: A Review," *Musical Quarterly* 52 (1966): 1–16, quotation on 14–15; Gordon Cyr, "Intervallic Structural Elements in Ives' Fourth Symphony," *Perspectives of New Music* 9 and 10 (1971): 291–303, quotation on 292.

20 Burkholder, *Charles Ives*. Perhaps the most frequently cited among the many books and essays that overstate the pervasiveness of Transcendentalism in Ives's life and thought is Rosalie S. Perry, *Charles Ives and the American Mind* (Kent, Ohio: Kent State University Press, 1974). The two most important studies of Ives and Transcendentalism are Burkholder, *Charles Ives* and Hertz, *Angels of Reality*.

21 Interestingly, in the Author's Preface (*Essays*, xxv) Ives offers a single year for the work, "Concord, Mass., 1845" (the year of George Ives's birth) rather than the 1840–60 time frame printed on the cover and title page of the published musical score.

2 Reception

1 A. Walter Kramer, "Pseudo-Literary Sonata!!!" *Musical America* 33 (April 2, 1921): 36; "Concord Unconquered," *Musical Courier* 82 (April 28, 1921): 22. Almost twenty years earlier the *Musical Courier* had positively (albeit not effusively) reviewed Ives's last major public offering, a performance of *The Celestial Country* on April 18, 1902. The reviews are reprinted in their entirety (compiled by Geoffrey Block), in *Charles Ives and His World*, ed. Burkholder, 278–88.

2 As noted in chapter 1, this dedication was removed from subsequent commercial editions of Ives's *Essays*.

3 The *Musical Courier* also noted Ives's musical borrowing, a practice that until relatively recently created a considerable obstacle to a positive reception of Ives. The borrowing which Ives, "consciously or unconsciously, lifted for his main theme" in "The Alcotts" is Charles Zeuner's *Missionary Chant*: "The late Zeuner, however, would be scandalized could he see his tune all undressed, as Charles [sic] has used it, with no proper bars no time nor anythin'."

4 Ernest Walker, "Review of Books" *Music & Letters* 2 (1921): 287–88, quotations on 288.

5 Edward [rightly Edwin] J. Stringham, "Ives Puzzles Critics With His Cubistic Sonata and 'Essays'," *Rocky Mountain News* (Denver), July 31, 1921, 1+, quotations on 17.

6 Henry Bellamann, "Concord, Mass., 1840–1860," 166–69, quotations from

these pages. For Ives's correspondence in 1921 with Bellamann concerning *Concord Sonata* see the letters in Ives Collection, Yale University Music Library, MSS, Box 27, Folder 8; reprinted letters, compiled and edited by Tom C. Owens, in *Charles Ives and His World*, ed. Burkholder, 214–17.

7 For a collection of essays that places Ives firmly in the mainstream of European classical music, see *Charles Ives and the Classical Tradition*, ed. Geoffrey Block and J. Peter Burkholder.

8 See also Sondra Rae Clark, "The Evolving *Concord Sonata*," and Clark, "Ives and the Assistant Soloist," *Clavier* 13, no. 7 (October, 1974): 17–20.

9 The fact that much of "Emerson" was derived from the orchestral *Emerson Overture* supports this view.

10 Although the flute part on the final two pages of "Thoreau" is optional and Ives offers a version for piano alone in both editions, in the performance notes for the second he writes that "Thoreau much prefers to hear the flute over Walden." In his "Thoreau" essay Ives mentions that the author of *Walden* played the flute and includes a hypothetical program of the movement in which "the poet's flute is heard out over the pond." *Essays*, 51 and 69.

11 William Lyon Phelps, "The Glorious Year A.D. Nineteen-Twenty," *Yale Alumni Weekly* 30 (December 17, 1920): 308.

12 Percy Goetschius: "I am absolutely convinced of your sincerity, and see many admirable evidences of that *logic*, which is a part of my pet Physical Law, in your work – note that I hesitate to call it 'Music' . . . As to your book, it is magnificent. . ." Ives, *Memos*, 192; the Goetschius and Hamilton letters are quoted in nn. 12 and 13.

13 Rossiter, *Charles Ives and His America*, 184–85; *Memos*, 99 (Mrs. Coolidge's letter to Harmony Ives quoted in n. 6).

14 Rossiter, *Charles Ives and His America*, 201.

15 Ibid., 197; "Music Club Hears Lecture Recital On Modern Sonata," *Atlanta Constitution*, January 5, 1922, 2.

16 Rossiter, *Charles Ives and His America*, 206–08. The origins of the often-quoted apocryphal story of Schmitz randomly wandering into the offices of Ives and Myrick to obtain life insurance in 1923 can be traced to Cowell and Cowell, *Charles Ives and His Music*, 101. See also Ronald V. Wiecki, "Two Musical Idealists – Charles Ives and E. Robert Schmitz: A Friendship Reconsidered," *American Music* 10 (Spring 1992): 1–19, especially 2–3 and Rossiter, *Charles Ives and His America*, 210–12.

17 Cowell's invitation of September 1930 to publish the *Concord Sonata* is reprinted in Rita Mead, *Henry Cowell's New Music 1925–1936: The Society, the Music Editions, and the Recordings* (Ann Arbor, Mich.: UMI Research

Press, 1981), 147. The Ives works published in *New Music* eventually included *A Set of Pieces for Theater or Chamber Orchestra* (1932), *Thirty-Four Songs* (1934), *Eighteen Songs* (1935), *Study No. 22* and *Three Protests* (1947), and *Lincoln, The Great Commoner* and *The Gong on the Hook and Ladder* (1953).

18   The following March Heyman played "Emerson" in a radio program broadcast by the Sorbonne Station of the Radio Institute of Paris. Geoffrey Block, *Charles Ives: A Bio-Bibliography*, 28, W65g.

19   Paul Rosenfeld, "Ives's Concord Sonata," 109–12.

20   Rosenfeld, "Charles E. Ives," *New Republic* 71 (July 20, 1932): 262–64.

21   Rosenfeld, *Discoveries of a Music Critic* (New York: Harcourt, Brace & Co., 1936), 315–24.

22   Rosenfeld, "Ives's Concord Sonata," 109–12.

23   Lawrence Gilman, "Music: A Masterpiece of American Music," 9. Gilman, the author of a seminal study on Edward MacDowell in 1905, had previously praised Ives in his review of the 1927 Fourth Symphony premiere (first and second movements): "This symphony has a sureness of touch which is not that of a neophyte learning an unfamiliar technique." *New York Herald Tribune*, January 31, 1927, 11.

24   Van Wyck Brooks, *The Flowering of New England 1815–1865* (New York: E. P. Dutton, 1936). As noted by Frank R. Rossiter, Gilman was only tangentially concerned with "the actual musical materials." Rossiter, *Charles Ives and His America*, 283.

25   In a letter of congratulations (February 27, 1939) William Lyon Phelps wrote that when he met Gilman at the opera the previous week the critic told him that Ives was "the greatest American composer of the past or present." Ives Collection, MSS 14, Box 31, Folder 6.

26   Ives lost a powerful and persuasive advocate when Gilman died early the following September, nine months after his *Concord Sonata* epiphany.

27   Irving Kolodin, "Pianist Plays Work By Ives," *New York Sun*, January 21, 1939.

28   John Sebastian [Goddard Lieberson], "Charles Ives at Last," *New Masses*, February 7, 1939, 30. During his tenure as president of Columbia Records (1955–66 and 1973–76) Lieberson did much to champion the recording of Ives's music.

29   See especially Larry Starr, *A Union of Diversities*.

30   Robert A. Simon, "American Music – Swing Drops In – Recitalists," *New Yorker* (January 28, 1939), 44–45.

31   "Insurance Man," *Time* (January 30, 1939), 44–45.

32   Carter, "The Case of Mr. Ives," 48–51.

33 Carter, "Expressionism and American Music," *Perspectives of New Music* 4 (Fall–Winter 1965): 1–3; repr. in *The Writings of Elliott Carter*, ed. Stone and Stone, 230–43.

34 Vivian Perlis, *Charles Ives Remembered*, 145.

35 Allen Edwards, *Flawed Words and Stubborn Sounds: A Conversation with Elliott Carter* (New York: W. W. Norton, 1971), 63. In the 1969 interview published in Perlis, *Charles Ives Remembered*, 131–45, Carter recalls that within a few years of writing his negative 1939 review ("in the mid-1940s"), he "began to think" that he "had been wrong about *Concord Sonata*," 139–40.

36 Ives wanted Kirkpatrick to prepare the second edition, but when it became clear that this would not be forthcoming, Ives took on this task himself (with the assistance in "Emerson" of his copyist George F. Roberts). See Block, "Remembrance of Dissonances Past." It should be noted that Frances Mullen, after performing "The Alcotts" and "Thoreau" in 1938 and inspired by the critical success of Kirkpatrick's January 20 premiere in Town Hall, played the entire sonata (using the first edition) shortly thereafter on June 25, 1939 at the Evenings on the Roof concerts in Los Angeles. On the fervent West Coast championing of Ives's *Concord Sonata* by Mullen and her husband Peter Yates from the late 1930s to the early 1950s, see Dorothy Lamb Crawford, *Evenings On and Off the Roof: Pioneering Concerts in Los Angeles 1939–1971* (Berkeley, Los Angeles, and London: University of California Press), 25, 33–34, 37–38, 47, 66, 92–93, and 119–21.

37 In contrast to his 1945 recording, which brings in elements which Ives shared from the still-unpublished second edition, Kirkpatrick's live Town Hall performance adheres exclusively to the first edition. See chapter 1, n. 5 and Block, "Remembrance of Dissonances Past."

38 As early as 1939, during his senior year at Harvard, Bernstein wrote appreciatively of Ives's idiosyncratic combination of a "New England style" and jazzy syncopations, "a most personal sound, different from the musical expression of any other composer." Leonard Bernstein, "The Absorption of Race Elements into American Music," Bachelor Thesis, Harvard University, 1939; repr. in *Findings* (New York: Doubleday, 1993), 37–100, quotation on 98.

39 Cowell and Cowell, *Charles Ives and His Music*, 4.

40 See chapter 4.

41 Cowell and Cowell, *Charles Ives and His Music*, 195.

42 Chase, *America's Music*.

43 H. Wiley Hitchcock, *Music in the United States: A Historical Introduction*

(Englewood Cliffs, New Jersey: Prentice-Hall, 1969; rev. 2nd edn, 1974; rev. 3rd edn, 1988), quotation on xi.

44 Wilfrid Mellers, *Music in a New Found Land: Themes and Developments in the History of American Music* (London: Barrie and Rockliff, 1964; rev. 2nd ed., 1987), 38–64, quotations on 48–49 and 56.

45 Carl Dahlhaus, *Nineteenth-Century Music*, trans. J. Bradford Robinson (Berkeley and Los Angeles, 1989), 386.

46 Charles Hamm, *Music in the New World* (New York and London: W. W. Norton, 1983), 424–37, quotation on 435.

47 Ibid., 435. Although Hamm devotes only one page to the *Concord Sonata*, Ives receives the principal emphasis in a chapter devoted to other American composers embarking on "the search for a national identity." At thirteen pages, Ives is granted more than three times the space reserved for the following composers: Edward MacDowell (4), Arthur Farwell (4), George Gershwin (4), Virgil Thomson (4), and Roy Harris (3). Aaron Copland is placed a distant second with five pages.

48 Among Ives's influential supporters was *New York Times* critic Harold C. Schonberg, who throughout his career regarded Ives (along with Louis Moreau Gottschalk) as one of America's "only two really nationalistic composers" and Ives alone as "the greatest of all American composers." See Schonberg, *Facing the Music* (New York: Summit Books, 1981), 128 and 147.

49 Perlis, *Charles Ives Remembered*, 220.

50 Thomas M. Brodhead, Preface to *Four Transcriptions from "Emerson"* (New York: Associated Music Publishers, forthcoming). One exception to this general rule occurs on the passage on page 9, systems 1–3: "These wide chords in RH were meant to (be) played as nearly as possible as one chord (together) and not as an arpeggio – And if the tempo is quite fast here the lower note may be omitted" (unpublished Performance Notes, Ives Collection, Yale University Music Library, Box 24, Folders 6 and 7). Brodhead also notes perceptively that the reverse is true of "Hawthorne." Unfortunately, Ives recorded only the first eleven seconds of this movement (May 11, 1938), a suggestive but inconclusive illustration of this principle (*Charles Ives: The 100th Anniversary*, Columbia M4 32504 [1974]). In contrast to Kirkpatrick's relatively brisk "Emerson," however, Ives's leisurely "Emerson" amply demonstrates Brodhead's generalization.

51 Kalish, formerly a principal pianist with the Boston Symphony Chamber Players, remains Head of Keyboard Activities at the Berkshire Music Center at Tanglewood and Artist-in-Residence at the State University of New York at Stony Brook. Hamelin is the 1985 winner of the Carnegie Hall International American Music Competition, and Blackwood is a distinguished

composer and theorist who has taught at the University of Chicago since
1958.

52 With the exception of the lesser-known American Music Award (won by
Hamelin, see note above), Ives enthusiasts will listen in vain to hear the
Concord Sonata in high-profile competitions. My own experience is that
conservatory-trained pianists, including those who regularly play challenging (if somewhat shorter) works such as the Carter Sonata or the Copland
Variations (and of course the Samuel Barber Sonata), tend to eschew Ives
piano sonatas and even his smaller keyboard works.

3 Genesis

1 Ives also dated his song *Thoreau*, which is based mainly on the "Down in the
corn field" material of the piano movement (see chapter 5), in 1915. It
appeared as no. 48 of the *114 Songs* in 1922.

2 Somewhat imprecisely, Ives locates the "two passages" on "p. 61–64–63"
(corresponding to pages 59–62–61 of the second edition).

3 Besides Emerson, Ives planned overtures based on Walt Whitman, Robert
Browning, and Matthew Arnold. The only overture that Ives completed,
however, was the *Robert Browning Overture.*

4 In his *Memos* (p. 77) Ives writes that the "Emerson" movement was conceived "as a male chorus, then overture or concerto for piano and orchestra,
and finally sonata." According to Ives, "the Emerson movement printed in
the piano book is a partial reduction for piano from the sketch of this concerto."

5 Carter quotation in Perlis, *Charles Ives Remembered*, 138.

6 In the Preface to his *Catalogue* Kirkpatrick wrote that "Ives's own dating,
even at the time of the event, is not always trustworthy." John Kirkpatrick, *A
Temporary Mimeographed Catalogue*, vii. At the Ives Centennial conference
in 1974 Kirkpatrick explained that Ives "had a very sly sense of humor and a
very acute New England sense of privacy," character traits that led to a situation in which "all datings in Ives are problematical." in *An Ives Celebration*,
ed. Hitchcock and Perlis, 69.

7 Solomon, "Some Questions of Veracity," 443–70.

8 Ibid., 463.

9 J. Peter Burkholder, "Charles Ives and His Fathers: A Response to Maynard
Solomon," *I.S.A.M. Newsletter* 18 (November 1988): 8–11, quotation on 11.

10 Ibid., 11. See also Wayne Shirley, "'The Second of July': A Charles Ives
Draft Considered as an Independent Work," in *A Celebration of American
Music: Words and Music in Honor of H. Wiley Hitchcock*, ed. Richard Craw-

ford, R. Allen Lott, and Carol J. Oja. (Ann Arbor: University of Michigan Press, 1990), 391–404.

11 J. Philip Lambert, "Communications," *Journal of the American Musicological Society* 42 (1989): 204–09, quotation on 208.

12 Carol K. Baron, "Dating Charles Ives's Music: Facts and Fictions," *Perspectives of New Music* 28 (1990): 20–56.

13 Ibid., 48–49.

14 Feder, *Charles Ives*, 351–57, quotations are from 353, 352, 357, 355, and 357, respectively.

15 Maynard Solomon, "Communications," *Journal of the American Musicological Society* 42 (1989): 209–18.

16 Unfortunately, the 1913 memo, like other memos, is now missing.

17 This revised copy R⁴, now housed, along with all the other *Concord Sonata* materials discussed in this volume, in the Ives Collection at Yale University, was the copy that Harmony Ives sent Lawrence Gilman in 1939. In the 1960s it was given to *New York Times* music critic Harold C. Schonberg, who eventually sent this considerably revised score to Yale in 1988. See Schonberg, "Don't Try to Please the Ladies, Rollo," *New York Times*, March 30, 1969, sec. 2, 19; repr. as "Ives: Compulsiveness, Complexity, Dissonance and Power," in *Facing the Music*, 147–51.

18 Solomon, "Communications," 215.

19 Sherwood, "The Choral Works of Charles Ives." I would like to thank Gayle Sherwood for sharing chapter 2 of this dissertation, "Dating Methodology and Data" (36–68), a typescript of her then forthcoming essay, "Questions and Veracities," 429–47, and her preliminary conclusions on the paper types and handwriting characteristics of the *Concord Sonata* papers.

20 Solomon, "Communications," 212. Sherwood explores the limitations of Kirkpatrick's sources, Ives's diaries and letters, lists of works, and "datable marginalia" in Ives's manuscripts. Concerning the latter (and most controversial) source, Sherwood, in contrast to both Kirkpatrick and Solomon, distinguishes between functional addresses with instructions for Ives's copyists and non-functional associative jottings "used to retrace stages in the development of a piece." In the end she discards this latter type of retrospective marginalia as unreliable. Sherwood, "Questions and Veracities," 433–34.

21 For the choral works, see Sherwood, "Questions and Veracities," 442; for the songs, see H. Wiley Hitchcock's forthcoming edition, for which Sherwood provided dates; and for the symphonies and violin sonatas, see Burkholder, *All Made of Tunes*, for which Sherwood provided preliminary dates.

22 Each manuscript has more than one identification, but they are most easily

accessed by their microfilm frame (or "f") numbers. The manuscripts for the *Concord Sonata* and related works are described in Kirkpatrick's *A Temporary Mimeographed Catalogue*, 31, 33, 42, 88–92, and 97–102.

23 According to Sherwood, the paper of Ives's ink copy of the *"Emerson" Transcriptions* was not produced until 1925, and the earliest date for the compositionally significant *Transcription* sketch (f4870), most likely 1926 (Sherwood, "The Choral Works of Charles Ives," 319). Furthermore, the presumably "functional" address and telephone number for copyist Emil Hanke, Cedar St NY 36653 John, ceased to be functional as of April 30, 1926. Although Ives recalled that the second, third, and fourth *Transcriptions* "were made a year or two after the Sonata was printed" (*Memos*, 202), all roads seem to converge on 1926 as a likelier date for these pieces as well.

24 Thomas M. Brodhead, "Ives's *Celestial Railroad* and His Fourth Symphony," 389–424. I am grateful to Thomas Brodhead for sharing a typescript of this paper and materials related to his forthcoming editions of *The Celestial Railroad* and *Four Transcriptions from "Emerson"* (New York: Associated Music Publishers).

25 Precise dates for post-first edition compositional activity are, like the various intertwining pre-first edition phases of the *Concord Sonata*, difficult to determine. In his 1935 letter to Kirkpatrick Ives recalled drafting the first *"Emerson" Transcription* between 1915 and 1918, and various *Celestial Railroad* sketches are extant on pre-1921 papers. Most of the surviving compositional activity for these works, however, utilizes the engraved first edition as a starting point since Ives's pencil or ink additions almost invariably appear on cut-up, pasted, or abbreviated copies of this edition. Also, see below n. 31.

26 For a more extensive comparison between the two *Concord Sonata* editions see Block, "Remembrance of Dissonances Past."

27 These Beethoven's Fifth Symphony statements occur near the end of system 2 (bass) on page 1 and the end of system 2 (treble) on page 16.

28 Three first edition notes refer to the sonata as a whole or to generalities of a particular movement: the interpretation of accidentals (p. 1); remarks on tempo and expression in "Hawthorne" (p. 21); and remarks on dynamics and pedaling in "Thoreau" (p. 61). The remaining notes refer to specific passages marked by asterisks on the following pages: p. 6, sys. 2; p. 18, sys. 4; p. 25, sys. 1–4; p. 40, sys. 5; and p. 68, sys. 3.

29 This note for a passage in "Hawthorne" (p. 46, sys. 5) is representative: "The octaves here need not be played literally, if in doing so the tempo is slowed up."

30 See for example the following in "Hawthorne" (p. 34, sys. 3): "Here the

Hymn for a moment is slightly held up by a Friendly Ghost in the Church Yard."

31 The Performance Notes are contained in Ives's Literary Writings in the Ives Collection at Yale University (Series II, A), Box 24, Folders 6 and 7 (f326–f449). They are fully transcribed in Clark, "The Evolving *Concord Sonata*," 356–75.

32 A particularly important note in this category clarifies the otherwise inexplicable meaning of the unusual V marks in "Emerson" (p. 3, sys. 2–4): "The notes with V mark are played almost but not quite together – a kind of quick upward accent." See the Performance Notes in the Ives Collection, f341 (in this instance a handwritten emendation on a typescript) and Ex. 5.2 ("Emerson," p. 3, sys. 3). For a handwritten (presumably earlier) variant on a draft that parenthetically specifies "the lowest first" see Clark, "The Evolving *Concord Sonata*," 360.

33 Since there is a pattern, according to Gayle Sherwood, that the extant sketches for the major instrumental works lie a few years after his own dates for the pieces, it may be that Ives's earlier dates conform to an early stage of each work, perhaps worked out by memory or notated on sketches that were discarded after being superseded.

34 Thanks to J. Peter Burkholder both for the idea and some of the specific content of this chronological summary.

4 Form and design

1 The passage is continued in chapter 6 of this handbook, p. 68. For more on J. Peter Burkholder's distinctions between "concert" music (e.g., sonatas) and the more experimental "research" music see Burkholder, *Charles Ives*, 49–50.

2 I am grateful to J. Peter Burkholder for identifying the extended fugue subject and for clarifying my interpretation of Ives's treatment of the *Tristan* motive.

3 Berger continues: "Pitch-class priority per se: 1) is not a sufficient condition of that music which is tonal, and 2) is compatible with music that is not tonally functional." Arthur Berger, "Problems of Pitch Organization in Stravinsky," *Perspectives of New Music* 2 (1963): 63. Berger's views on non-functional tonality are quoted and applied to Alban Berg's *Wozzeck* in George Perle, *The Operas of Alban Berg. Volume One/Wozzeck* (Berkeley, Los Angeles, and London: University of California Press, 1980): 131.

4 The programmatic implications of this bitonality will be noted in chapter 6, p. 75.

5 For more detailed harmonic analysis see Thomas Russel Albert, "The Harmonic Language of Charles Ives' *Concord Sonata*." D.M.A. diss., University of Illinois, 1974.

6 For another interpretation of the form in "Hawthorne" see John Kirkpatrick, "Preface," in Charles E. Ives, *Symphony No. 4* (New York and London: Associated Music Publishers, 1965), vii. Kirkpatrick's seven-part arch-like division (phantasmagoria–nocturne–ragtime–contrasts–ragtime–nocturne–phantasmagoria) is detailed in Thomas M. Brodhead, "Ives's *Celestial Railroad* and His Fourth Symphony," 419–21. See also Burkholder, *All Made of Tunes*, 353.

7 For a motivic analysis of "Emerson" see Ann Ghander, "Charles Ives: Organisation in *Emerson*," *Musicology: The Journal of the Musicological Society of Australia* 6 (1980): 111–27. A useful introduction to Ives's practice of "developing variation" in "Emerson" is found in Keith C. Ward, "Ives, Schoenberg, and the Musical Ideal," in *Charles Ives and the Classical Tradition*, ed. Block and Burkholder, 98–99.

8 For a worthwhile overview and interpretation of Ives's diverse contrapuntal techniques and purposes see J. Philip Lambert, "Ives and Counterpoint," *American Music* 9 (1991): 119–48.

9 For a thoughtful interpretation of Ives's formal and stylistic divisions in "The Alcotts" see Larry Starr, "Charles Ives: The Next Hundred Years – Towards a Method of Analyzing the Music," *Music Review* 38 (1977): 101–11. See also Burkholder, *All Made of Tunes*, 195–200.

10 For a detailed motivic analysis of "Thoreau" see Robert Douglas Fruehwald, "Motivic Transformation in the 'Thoreau' Movement of Charles Ives' *Concord Sonata*."

11 Cowell and Cowell, *Charles Ives and His Music*, 201.

5 Borrowing

1 The first to notice Ives's predilection to select his borrowed material for their common properties was probably Henry Bellamann in his Fourth Symphony program notes for *Pro Musica*, January 29, 1927. Two important later studies that develop this idea are Marshall, "Charles Ives's Quotations: Manner or Substance?" and Cyr, "Intervallic Structural Elements in Ives' Fourth Symphony," 291–303.

2 The major study of all aspects of Ives's borrowing is J. Peter Burkholder, *All Made of Tunes*, a considerably reworked expansion of the middle third of his dissertation, "The Evolution of Charles Ives's Music: Aesthetics, Quotation, Technique" (Ph.D. diss., University of Chicago, 1983). The literature

on European musical borrowing constitutes a large and rapidly growing field. For a useful introduction to some of the broader issues (along with several well-chosen examples drawn from the music of Brahms) see Charles Rosen, "Influence: Plagiarism and Inspiration," *19th Century Music* 2 (1978): 87–100. Classical and vernacular borrowings by Ives's New England predecessors, including those used by his Yale composition professor Horatio Parker, are discussed by William K. Kearns, *Horatio Parker, 1863–1919* (Metuchen, N.J.: Scarecrow Press, 1990), 241–43, and Nicholas Tawa, "Ives and the New England School," in *Charles Ives and the Classical Tradition*, ed. Block and Burkholder, 51–72.

3 Burkholder, *All Made of Tunes*. For an introduction to Ives's borrowing practices and their historical context the following essays by Burkholder are highly recommended: "'Quotation' and Emulation: Charles Ives's Uses of His Models," *Musical Quarterly* 71 (Winter 1985): 1–26; "Quotation and Paraphrase in Ives's Second Symphony," *Nineteenth Century Music* 11 (1987): 3–25; "The Uses of Existing Music: Musical Borrowing as a Field," *Music Library Association Notes* 50 (1994): 851–70; and "Ives and the Nineteenth-Century European Tradition," in *Charles Ives and the Classical Tradition*, ed. Block and Burkholder, 11–33.

4 On the programmatic content of the *Concord Sonata* see Burkholder, *All Made of Tunes*, 350–57 and chapter 6 below.

5 Ives, *Essays*, 36 and *Concord Sonata*, 2nd edn [74; pages of *Concord Sonata* are unnumbered after p. 68, having counted them myself, they are given hereafter in square brackets].

6 Incipits and other useful information about many of the borrowings cited in this chapter can be found in Clayton W. Henderson, *The Charles Ives Tunebook*. See table on pp. 61–64.

7 Allen Gimbel, "Elgar's Prize Song: Quotation and Allusion in the Second Symphony," *19th Century Music* 12 (1989): 233.

8 "Concord Unconquered," 22.

9 *A History of Music* (New York: Harcourt, Brace and Company, 1935), 645.

10 Carter, "The Case of Mr. Ives," 48–51.

11 Ibid., 51. In his personal first edition copy of the *Concord Sonata* (R⁹), now housed along with Ives's revised and annotated first edition copies in the Ives Collection, Yale Music Library, R¹–R¹⁷, Carter labeled the *Martyn* passage "Hymn of Pilgrims" (first ed., p. 33) and the *Country Band March* on the next page "Band at Vanity Fair." Both references refer to Hawthorne's story *The Celestial Railroad*. The reference to Pilgrims is taken from Henry Bellamann's program notes for the *Pro Musica* premiere of the Fourth Symphony (first and second movements) in 1927 (see note 1) and repeated in Ives's

prefatory remarks to the publication of the second movement, "Notes on Fourth Symphony," *New Music* 2, no. 1 (January 1929). See also Kirkpatrick, "Preface" to Ives, *Symphony No. 4*, vii–x.

12 Cowell and Cowell, *Charles Ives and His Music*, 190–201.

13 Ibid., 199; Kirkpatrick, *A Temporary Mimeographed Catalogue*, 90; Henderson, *The Charles Ives Tunebook*.

14 Personal communication from John Kirkpatrick in 1971.

15 Kirkpatrick, *A Temporary Mimeographed Catalogue*, 89.

16 Ibid., 90.

17 The principal figure in "Pig Town Fling" does, however, share the descending major second–minor third intervallic progression of motive *u* (Ex. 4.1 a). See table on p. 63.

18 Kirkpatrick, *A Temporary Mimeographed Catalogue*, 88 and 97. "Emerson" (p. 1, sys. 2) is clearly derived from a passage in *Study No. 9* (p. 14, sys. 5–p. 15, sys. 1), ed. Henry Cowell, Merion Music, 1949; repr. 1975.

19 A transposed version of Bach's name also opens Ives's *Three Page Sonata*.

20 According to Fruehwald, the pun is this: the six-note opening of *Bethany* (B-A-G-G-E-E) is paraphrased with rhythmic and transpositional liberties by Ives as B-A-G-[eight intervening notes]-D#-C-C (last three treble pitches at the end of p. 62, sys. 5 and continued on p. 63, sys. 1 [incorrectly noted in Fruehwald as p. 63, sys. 5]). Robert Douglas Fruehwald, "Motivic Transformation in the 'Thoreau' Movement," 33.

21 Brodhead, "Ives's *Celestial Railroad* and His Fourth Symphony," 392. In *The Charles Ives Tunebook* Henderson designates "Peter, Peter, Pumpkin Eater" as Unknown Tune H201.

22 The other Debussy prelude borrowings suggested by Hertz are *Bruyères* and *Des Pas sur la neige*. David Michael Hertz, *Angels of Reality*, 106–111.

23 John Jeffrey Gibbens, "Debussy's Impact on Ives: An Assessment" (D.M.A. diss., University of Illinois at Urbana-Champaign, 1985).

24 Thanks to J. Peter Burkholder for the Musorgsky and Rimsky-Korsakov references and to Julian Rushton for the Debussy.

25 The use of this bitonal juxtaposition in "Thoreau" is noted in Felix Meyer, *"The Art of Speaking Extravagantly,"* 173.

26 See also Clark, "The Evolving *Concord Sonata*," 158.

27 In the *Emerson Overture* Ives assigns this melody to a trumpet (Ives Collection, Yale University, fo565). For a facsimile of this page see Sondra Rae Clark, "The Element of Choice in Ives's *Concord Sonata*," 170.

28 See also *Memos*, 46 and 246–47.

29 Ibid., Appendix 4, nos. 61 (*Nature's Way*), 68 (*Ilmenau*), and 79 (*Rosamunde*), 172–73. In an insert for a second edition of the *Essays* "if there

happen to be one" (*Essays*, 253) Ives expressed his admiration for Schubert as a composer of substantive songs.

30 The New Haven Symphony repertoire performed during Ives's years at Yale is listed in David Eiseman, "Charles Ives and the European Symphonic Tradition: A Historic Reappraisal" (Ph.D. diss., University of Illinois, 1972), 266–69.

31 Daniel Gregory Mason, *The Romantic Composers* (New York: Macmillan, 1906; repr. 1930), 100–01.

32 The fact that the seventh through ninth notes of Schubert's melody (transposed), as they appear in "The Alcotts" D-B♭-C (p. 54, sys. 1) and transposed again on system 2 (A♭-F-G) are the same as the *Martyn* fragment could be used to support an argument either for excluding or embracing this speculative reference.

33 I am grateful to J. Peter Burkholder for this last insight.

34 Charles Rosen, "Radical, Conventional Mozart," *The New York Review of Books* (December 19, 1991): 56. Rosen makes a similar point in *The Frontiers of Meaning: Three Informal Lectures on Music* (New York: Hill and Wang, 1994), 97–98.

35 The extensive reuse of "Emerson" in *Four Transcriptions from "Emerson"* is not included among the self-borrowings in Appendix 1. *Transcription No. 1* includes page 1 through page 2, sys. 1 (in addition to an extended passage derived from the *Emerson Overture*), *No. 2* corresponds to pages 6–11, *No. 3* parallels page 14, sys. 3, measure 3 through page 16, sys. 4, and *No. 4* corresponds to page 17, sys. 4 through page 19. In most cases the material of the *Transcriptions* is used as the foundation of the parallel passage in the second edition of the *Concord Sonata* (see chapter 3, pp. 27–28).

36 The self-borrowings below do not encompass the derivations from the Fourth Symphony (second movement) and the transformed use of analogous musical material in *The Celestial Railroad*. See Brodhead, "Ives's *Celestial Railroad* and the Fourth Symphony," for a comprehensive correspondence among the three "Hawthorne" movements, 392–93.

37 James J. Fuld, *The World Book of World-Famous Music: Classical, Popular and Folk* (New York: Crown Publishers, 1966), 278.

6 The Program

1 Daniel Gregory Mason, *Contemporary Composers* (New York: The Macmillan Company, 1918), 83.

2 Ibid., 84.

3 For other evidence that "Mason's thought clearly influenced Ives's essays"

see Frank R. Rossiter, "The 'Genteel Tradition' in American Music," *Journal of American Culture* 4 (1981): 107–15, especially 113–14. Ives also demonstrated his independence of Mason's views, for example when he contradicts Mason's description of Strauss's comedy as "Meredithian." For Ives, "Meredith is a little too deep or too subtle for Strauss, unless it be granted that cynicism is more a part of comedy than a part of refined insult" (*Essays*, 87).

4 An "insert" for a new edition of the *Essays* ("if there happen to be one") is included in *Essays*, 253, n. 52.

5 Nicholas Temperley, "The *Symphonie Fantastique* and Its Program," *Musical Quarterly* 57 (1971): 593–608, quotation on 601–02.

6 Ibid., 602.

7 Berlioz, quoted ibid., 595.

8 Berlioz, quoted ibid., 603.

9 Ives Collection, Yale University Music Library, R^1–R^{17}.

10 *Concord Sonata*, 2nd ed. [73–74]. See chapter 3, n. 31. The unpublished Performance Notes on the *Concord Sonata*, Ives Collection, Yale University Music Library, Box 24, Folders 6 and 7 are reprinted in Clark, "The Evolving *Concord Sonata*," 356–75.

11 See Ralph Waldo Emerson, *The Complete Works*, Centenary Edition, 12 vols. (Boston: Houghton Mifflin Company, 1903–04).

12 See, for example, Victor Fell Yellin's review of Ives's *Essays*, *Journal of the American Musicological Society* 17 (1964): 229–31.

13 In another unpublished performance note Ives wrote that "*Bottom Page 14* may be something of the way that Emerson would hit out from the shoulder whether in an abolitionist riot or a drastic sermon in Concord" (Ives Collection, f328, f332, f348, and f353 [the word 'drastic' is a handwritten emendation added to f348]). The latter version is reprinted in Clark, "The Evolving *Concord Sonata*," 365. The published notes place a more Transcendental slant on the music from the bottom of page 14. The hitting "out from the shoulder" (p. 14, sys. 5, m. 2) is now interpreted as "but one of Emerson's sudden calls for a Transcendental Journey." The unpublished notes for pages 15–18 (on the same as above) share this theme as they describe music which tries "to emulate Emerson's vigorous and transcendent climb to the Eternal Mountain tops."

14 Feder, *Charles Ives*, 262.

15 Although in the second edition he does not label this passage "verse" in the score, Ives included the following performance note: "Here begins a section which may reflect some of Emerson's poetry rather than the prose." 2nd edn [73].

16 Section 2 clearly evolves into "prose" material that is not so labeled by Ives in the first edition; the composer does, however, acknowledge the change from prose to verse (after three systems) in section 7.

17 Felix Meyer posits numerous additional connections and parallels between the *Essays* and the sonata throughout *"The Art of Speaking Extravagantly."*

18 "It is this underlying courage of the purest humility that gives Emerson that outward aspect of serenity which is felt to so great an extent in much of his work, especially in his codas and perorations" (*Essays*, 35).

19 Perlis, *Charles Ives Remembered*, 218. The other quoted material in this paragraph is also taken from p. 218. J. Peter Burkholder credits Harmony Ives for influencing her husband's turn to his literary and historical past for musical subject matter. See Burkholder, *Charles Ives*, 95–101.

20 The correlation between Ives's description in his *Essays* (42) and the score goes something like this: "It ['Hawthorne'] might have something to do with the children's excitement on that 'frosty Berkshire morning, and the frost imagery on the enchanted hall window" (p. 21, sys. 1–p. 22, sys. 2); "... or something to do with 'The Celestial Railroad'" (p. 22, sys. 3); "... or something to do with 'Feathertop,' the scarecrow, and his 'looking Glass' and 'the little demons dancing around his pipe bowl' (p. 23, end of sys. 2); "... or something to do with the old hymn-tune that haunts the church and sings only to those in the churchyard to protect them from secular noises as when the circus parade comes down Main Street" (pp. 34–37); "... or the 'Slave's Shuffle'" (p. 37, sys. 1). Ives offers other references to stories that cannot be reliably associated with musical passages. These include "the concert at the Stamford camp meeting," "the Concord he-nymph," and the stories "The Seven Vagabonds," "Circe's Palace," "something else in *The Wonder Book*," or "Phoebe's Garden" in the novel *The House of Seven Gables*. The verification of these references as well as Kirkpatrick's plausible but speculative locations of the "Slave's Shuffle," remains problematic.

21 These include notes for the following pages of the second edition: p. 33, system 1; p. 34, sys. 3–4; p. 34, sys. 5, m. 2; and p. 36, sys. 5.

22 In the 1913 memo, for example, Ives describes "distant bells" heard "in the old churchyard." An unpublished performance note specifies that these church bells are "the group of chords in the right hand staff of Page 25" (i.e., the chords played by the strip of board) (Ives Collection, f372 in the version quoted above, variants on f335 and f381). Another unpublished performance note (Ives Collection, f336), explains that the sixteenth rest in the hymn passage (p. 34, sys. 3, m. 1) is intended to "reflect a slight start which the graveyard ghosts occasionally gave to the cemetery angels while singing."

(These unpublished performance notes are also reprinted in Clark, "The Evolving *Concord Sonata*," 367–68.)

Additional support for the descriptions in the 1913 "memo" and the "Hawthorne" essay is found in two revised first edition copies. In R^{14} (old designation R^{12}) the passage is labeled "Demons around Pipe rim" and in R^6 (old designation R^5) Ives designated the right-hand part "Demons" and the left-hand "Pipe rim" (*Memos*, 81 and Clark, "The Evolving *Concord Sonata*," 199). For those unfamiliar with Hawthorne's story "Feathertop," the principal character, Mother Rigby, gives the title character (a scarecrow) a magical pipe that will be lit by demons.

23 *Memos*, 81. The first missing page is supplied by Elliott Carter, who wrote "Celestial Railroad" in his personal first edition copy (R^9) at the beginning of p. 22, sys. 3.

24 Brodhead, "Ives's *Celestial Railroad* and His Fourth Symphony," 389–424; especially 394–96 and the programmatic synopsis on 419–22. For a helpful discussion of the programmatic relevance in Fourth Symphony and *The Celestial Railroad* borrowings see Burkholder, *All Made of Tunes*, 357–60 and 389–410, respectively.

25 Kirkpatrick, "Preface" to Ives, *Symphony No. 4*, 392–93. See also Bellamann, "The Music of Charles Ives," 16–22, and Ives, "Notes on Fourth Symphony." For a contemporary edition of Hawthorne's story see *Hawthorne's Works*, 13 vols. (Boston: Houghton Mifflin, 1882).

26 In addition to the "Celestial Railroad" rubric on p. 22 (see n. 23), Carter made two other annotations of a programmatic nature: "Hymn of Pilgrims" (p. 33, sys. 2) and "Band at Vanity Fair" (p. 34, sys. 3, m. 3). See p. 99 n. 11.

27 Ives responds: "In neither the Emerson or Thoreau movements are there any quotations or attempts to picture any particular essay or saying or philosophic part. They try rather to reflect the underlying definite and indefinite things in the author's characters and works – or, as suggested in the preface, but composite pictures, or an impression" (*Memos*, 199).

28 See, for example, the programmatic interpretation of the "high small notes" on pages 55–56: "They are but a kind of overtone echoes over the 'Orchard House' elms." Performance Note for the second edition, [73].

29 In this section the "Loch Lomond" paraphrase is one reasonably clear example of a Scottish song, and the other contemporary borrowed fragments, the *Wedding March* from Wagner's *Lohengrin* (1850) and the minstrel song, A. F. Winnemore's "Stop That Knocking at My Door" (1843), might have been played on the Alcotts' spinet (see chapter 5).

30 Although the "human faith melody" is heard in its complete state at the end of the first section, it is only in its second statement at the conclusion of the

final section that the "sonorous" hymn-like expression captures the "common sentiment" as well as the "strength of hope" and "the power of the common soul."

31 Henry David Thoreau, *The Variorum Walden*, annotated by Walter Harding (New York: Washington Square Press, 1966), 83. Harding notes that this passage "is one of the most famous in *Walden* and is considered by many to be one of the outstanding expressions of the mystical experience in literature" (*Walden*, 283). For a contemporary edition of Thoreau see *The Writings of Henry David Thoreau*, Walden Edition, 20 vols. (Boston: Houghton Mifflin Company, 1906).

32 Ives's attitudes towards Debussy are admirably explored in Hertz, *Angels of Reality*, 97–98, 100–02, and 105–11.

33 Thoreau refers to his flute in two passages of *Walden* (*The Variorum Walden*, 117 and 169).

34 Feder, *Charles Ives*, 270–71.

35 In Ives's diary entry for January 22, 1919 the composer wrote in his own hand, "C. [harlie] worked on Thoreau. – trying to write something to make people think Thoreau movement sounds like Thoreau." D8 in the Ives Collection, Yale University Music Library, Series V, Box 45, Folder 8. Cited in Burkholder, *Charles Ives*, 145, n. 2.

36 In an unpublished performance note Ives also offers a programmatic explanation for the final sounds of his sonata: "This is but Walden dying towards Eternity. Before the last C# in the left hand sounds over the mountains, it is hoped that the three notes in the right hand sky and the lower D major still be faintly heard as the C# sings Good-night" (Ives Collection, f340, f379, and f388 are identical for this quotation. Reprinted with variant versions in Clark, "The Evolving *Concord Sonata*," 375).

37 Cowell and Cowell, *Charles Ives and His Music*, 147.

38 Jacques Barzun, *Berlioz and the Romantic Century*, 2 vols., 3rd edn (New York and London: Columbia University Press, 1969) I, 162 and Gerald Abraham, *A Hundred Years of Music*, 2nd edn (London: Duckworth, 1949), cited in Temperley, "The *Symphonie fantastique* and its Program," 593. Sixteen years after Cowell, Gordon Cyr, writing about Ives's Fourth Symphony, similarly dismisses the tendency to offer an "extramusical rationale for Ives's novel structures" when "a perfectly valid *musical* justification" would suffice. Cyr, "Intervallic Structural Elements in Ives' Fourth Symphony," 291–303; quotations on 291–92.

39 *Letters of Felix Mendelssohn-Bartholdy, from 1833 to 1847*, ed. Paul Mendelssohn-Bartholdy and Carl Mendelssohn-Bartholdy (London: Longman, Green, Longman, Roberts, and Green, 1863), 298. Hector

Berlioz, Preface to *Roméo et Juliette* (1839); see Julian Rushton, *Berlioz: Roméo et Juliette* (Cambridge University Press, 1994), 88.

40 A pioneering and central figure in this challenge to music's autonomy is Susan McClary. See especially her *Feminine Endings: Music, Gender, and Sexuality* (Minneapolis, Minn.: University of Minnesota Press, 1991). For a more direct application to Ives see Judith Tick, "Charles Ives and Gender Ideology," in *Musicology and Difference: Gender and Sexuality in Music Scholarship*, ed. Ruth A. Solie (Berkeley: University of California Press, 1993), 83–106.

Select bibliography

Standard reference works, biographies, and musical studies of Ives

Block, Geoffrey. *Charles Ives: A Bio-Bibliography*. New York: Greenwood Press, 1988.

Block, Geoffrey and J. Peter Burkholder, eds. *Charles Ives and the Classical Tradition*. New Haven: Yale University Press, 1996.

Burkholder, J. Peter. *Charles Ives: The Ideas Behind the Music*. New Haven: Yale University Press, 1985.

All Made of Tunes: Charles Ives and the Uses of Musical Borrowing. New Haven: Yale University Press, 1995.

Burkholder, J. Peter, ed. *Charles Ives and His World*. Princeton, N.J.: Princeton University Press, 1996.

See also Block.

Cowell, Henry and Sidney Cowell. *Charles Ives and His Music*. New York: Oxford University Press, 1955; 2nd edn, 1969.

Feder, Stuart. *Charles Ives: "My Father's Song": A Psycho-Analytic Biography*. New Haven: Yale University Press, 1992.

Henderson, Clayton W. *The Charles Ives Tunebook*. Bibliographies in American Music, 14. Warren, Mich.: Harmonie Park Press, 1990.

Hertz, David Michael. *Angels of Reality: Emersonian Unfoldings in Wright, Stevens, and Ives*. Carbondale and Edwardsville: Southern Illinois University Press, 1993.

Hitchcock, H. Wiley. *Ives: A Survey of the Music*. London: Oxford University Press, 1977.

Hitchcock, H. Wiley and Vivian Perlis, eds. *An Ives Celebration: Papers and Panels of the Ives Centennial Festival–Conference*. Urbana: University of Illinois Press, 1977.

Ives, Charles. *Essays Before a Sonata, The Majority, and Other Writings*, ed. Howard Boatwright. New York: W. W. Norton, 1970.

Memos, ed. John Kirkpatrick. New York: W. W. Norton, 1972.

Kirkpatrick, John. *A Temporary Mimeographed Catalogue of the Music Manuscripts and Related Materials of Charles Edward Ives 1874–1954*. New Haven: Library of the Yale School of Music, 1960; repr. 1973.

"Ives, Charles (Edward)," in *The New Grove Dictionary of American Music*, ed. H. Wiley Hitchcock and Stanley Sadie. 4 vols. London: Macmillan, 1986, II, 503–20.

See also Ives.

Lambert, Philip, ed. *Ives Studies*. Cambridge: Cambridge University Press, forthcoming.

Perlis, Vivian, *Charles Ives Remembered: An Oral History*. New Haven: Yale University Press, 1974.

Perlis, Vivian, ed., *Charles Ives Papers*, Yale University Archival Collection MSS 14. New Haven: Yale University Press, 1983.

See also Hitchcock.

Rathert, Wolfgang. *The Seen and Unseen: Studien zum Werk von Charles Ives*. Berliner Musikwissenschaftliche Arbeiten, ed. Carl Dahlhaus and Rudolf Stephan. Vol. 38. Munich and Salzburg: Emil Katzbichler, 1991.

Rossiter, Frank R. *Charles Ives and His America*. New York: Liveright, 1975.

Sinclair, James B. *The Descriptive Catalogue of the Music of Charles Ives*. New Haven: Yale University Press, forthcoming.

Sinclair, James B., comp. *The John Kirkpatrick Papers*. New Haven, Conn., November 1993.

Starr, Larry. *A Union of Diversities: Style in the Music of Charles Ives*. New York: Schirmer Books, 1992.

Swafford, Jan. *Charles Ives: A Life With Music*. New York: W.W. Norton, 1996.

Studies of the *Concord Sonata*

Albert, Thomas Russel. "The Harmonic Language of Charles Ives' *Concord Sonata*." D.M.A. diss., University of Illinois, 1974.

Block, Geoffrey. "Ives and the 'Sounds That Beethoven Didn't Have'," in *Charles Ives and the Classical Tradition*, ed. Block and Burkholder, 34–50.

"Remembrance of Dissonances Past: The Two Published Editions of Ives's *Concord Sonata*," in *Ives Studies*, ed. Lambert.

Brodhead, Thomas M. "Ives's *Celestial Railroad* and His Fourth Symphony." *American Music* 12 (1994): 389–424.

Chmaj, Betty E. "Sonata for American Studies: Perspectives on Charles Ives." *Prospects: An Annual of American Culture Studies* 4 (1979): 1–58.

"Charles Ives and the Concord Sonata," in *Poetry and the Fine Arts: Papers from the Poetry Sessions of the European Association for American Studies*

Biennial Conference, Rome 1984, ed. Roland Hagenbüchle and Jaqueline S. Ollie. Regensburg: Friedrich Pustet, 1989, 37–60.

Clark, Sondra Rae. "The Evolving *Concord Sonata*: A Study of Choices and Variants in the Music of Charles Ives." Ph.D. diss., Stanford University, 1972.

"The Element of Choice in Ives's *Concord Sonata*." *Musical Quarterly* 60 (1974): 167–86.

Conen, Hermann. "'All the Wrong Notes are Right.' Zu Charles Ives' 2. Klaviersonate 'Concord, Mass., 1840–60'." *Neuland* 1 (1980): 28–42.

Crutchfield, Will. "The 'Concord' Sonata: An American Masterpiece." *Opus* 1, no. 4 (June 1985): 21–22+.

Fisher, Fred. *Ives' Concord Sonata*. Denton, Tex.: C/G Productions, 1981.

Fruehwald, Robert Douglas. "Motivic Transformation in the 'Thoreau' Movement of Charles Ives' *Concord Sonata*." Ph.D. diss., Washington University, 1985.

Ghander, Ann. "Charles Ives: Organisation in *Emerson*." *Musicology: The Journal of the Musicological Society of Australia* 6 (1980): 111–27.

Kirkpatrick, John. Jacket notes for *Concord Sonata* recording. Columbia MS-7192 (1968).

Kramer, Lawrence. "A Completely New Set of Objects," in his *Music and Poetry: The Nineteenth Century and After*. Berkeley and Los Angeles: University of California Press, 1984, 171–202.

Meyer, Felix. *"The Art of Speaking Extravagantly": Eine vergleichende Studie der* Concord Sonata *und der* Essays Before a Sonata *von Charles Ives*. Der Schweizerischen Musikforschenden Gesellschaft, series II, vol. 34. Bern and Stuttgart: Paul Hapt, 1991.

Schubert, Giselher. "Die Concord-Sonata von Charles Ives. Anmerkungen zur Werkstruktur und Interpretation," in *Aspeckte der musikalischen Interpretation. Festschrift z. 70 Geburtstag von Sava Savoff*, ed. Hermann Danuser. Hamburg: K. D. Wagner, 1980, 121–38.

Starr, Larry. "Charles Ives: The Next Hundred Years – Towards a Method of Analyzing the Music." *Music Review* 38 (1977): 101–11.

Index